WHERE
THE
HEART
RESIDES

DAISY ANN HICKMAN

EAGLE BROOK
WILLIAM MORROW
AND COMPANY, INC.
NEW YORK

WHERE THE HEART RESIDES

Timeless Wisdom
of the
American Prairie

PUBLISHED BY EAGLE BROOK
AN IMPRINT OF WILLIAM MORROW AND COMPANY, INC.
1350 AVENUE OF THE AMERICAS, NEW YORK, N.Y. 10019

Library of Congress Cataloging-in-Publication Data has been applied for.
ISBN 0-688-16884-1

Printed in the United States of America
First Edition
1 2 3 4 5 6 7 8 9 10

BOOK DESIGN BY DEBORAH KERNER

www.williammorrow.com

For unseen powers—
may they guide us wisely and well
in our earthly journey;

for friends, family, and angels
who light our way;

for Anna and James,
may they know eternal love . . .
may our hearts remember always.

CONTENTS

ACKNOWLEDGMENTS

As the perfect culmination of my life's journey to this point, this book has created the wisest union of all by joining my love of words to the endearing prairie and its people, by connecting the loose threads of my life while inspiring a few beginnings, as well. I want to thank everyone who made this project come to life in such a magnificent way.

Michelle Toki Shinseki, the guiding light behind this endeavor, one of the first to catch a glimpse of its promise and purpose, is at the top of my list. A gifted editor, she shared her enthusiasm and abilities unconditionally, offering the right touch at just the right moment.

Bob H. Miller, photographer, provided his talents, his artistic vision, with exceptional concern and regard for the demands of the project. A fellow graduate of Riggs High School, this book became an unexpected opportunity for Bob and me to turn back the pages of time.

Matthew G. Rosenberger, entertainment lawyer and star pitcher for the Woodland Giants, practices law in Philadelphia; an inspired *and* inspiring attorney, Matt is a life force of meaningful distinction.

Special thanks to Frances Jones, Peter Harper, John Rhoads, and everyone who contributed their time and thoughts to this project. And to all of you who read this book, I am especially grateful. From cover to cover, it was written for *you* —the "pioneers of the twenty-first century."

The verie instant

that I saw you,

did my heart flie

to your service.

—WILLIAM
SHAKESPEARE,
The Tempest

Over all, rocks, wood, and water, brooded the spirit of repose, and the silent energy of nature stirred the soul to its inmost depths.

—THOMAS COLE (1801–1848),
Essay on American Society, 1835

INTRODUCTION:
A Dance with Destiny—
Growing up Prairie Wise

Everyone knows what it means to grow up streetwise. Yet only a handful are familiar with what it means to grow up "prairie wise"—a new concept perhaps, one that seems a bit puzzling and rather antiquated. Things like prairie chicken (grouse), prairie dog, prairie schooner (wagon), even prairie wolf (coyote), paint a vivid picture, even today, while "prairie wise" sounds strange and foreign—an idea pertaining to the pioneer era, an idea whose time has come and gone. Surely contemporary society, in its advanced and sophisticated state, conquered and moved well beyond the prairie mentality many, many years ago. And wisely so.

Given the urbanization of America since the time of the pioneers, that is indeed how it seems—on the surface.

Yet wisdom, a primary subject of this book, lives in the heart and soul, not on the surface, so, if we are to rediscover the true power of heart in our lives, we must look beneath the obvious for answers. Like curious children, we must peer into the lives of our forefathers, as some aspects of the pioneer and prairie creed live on in all of us.

Indeed, we must not settle for surface explanations or assumptions: The answers are rarely that sheer, seldom that vitreous.

In digging for solutions to problems that plague our world at the turn of the century, we must venture into the new millennium like spirited and dedicated explorers; we must move beyond conventional thinking by considering the old from a powerful new perspective: We must become prairie wise.

The prairie lands have come to represent our heritage as a people, our history as a nation—one that was built on the strength of the pioneer spirit, for it was that sense of adventure and clear purpose that moved our country forward into the twentieth century. Therefore, I cannot imagine a better place to look for inspiration, guidance, and clues to our survival as we greet the twenty-first century. Because in our search for new solutions to today's dilemmas we may have forgotten to consider what we already know; we may have forgotten to listen to our hearts.

But the past lives on in all of us; we can reclaim what is rightfully ours. It is just a matter of revisiting the lands, indeed, the place, which willingly opened its arms to those who traveled before us. Our journey, however, will not be a physical one, nor will we ride in a covered wagon. Clearly, we will not confront dust storms, blizzards, or prairie rattlesnakes. Our pilgrimage will be a spiritual and emotional journey undertaken with hope, heart, and love. By returning to a place that has moved so many to tears, for one reason or another, as we move forward together bravely and with searching hearts, the prairie spirit will somehow come alive in each of us.

It is a commendable goal filled with dignity and pride, but, perhaps, it is easier for me. I grew up there—in the middle of nowhere, a common reference for the prairie—and for some reason spent a good deal of time contemplating the meaning of life, good versus evil, the purpose and simple grandeur of nature, heavenly spirits and higher powers, the overwhelming beauty of mature wheat fields and great stretches of deep, clear water. And while I did not fully understand the true value of my experiences until later in life, I could feel the prairie's pull on my soul no matter how far away I drifted.

Like a poetic image, a magnetic force, the South Dakota prairie had wormed its way into my heart in a way that defied logic and understanding. With that as my puzzle, I continued to ponder the prairie, its beauty and place in the world, its people and culture, until one day I began to piece it all together. A sort of prairie wisdom, a philosophy of life, emerged, and soon thereafter began to take the shape of a book that could be made relevant to the broader society at the turn of the century.

Inspired by love—for a place that is distinctive yet down-to-earth, by a desire to share my thoughts with those who seek greater harmony and joy in their own lives—a rough outline turned into paragraphs, then pages, and eventually, several years later, into this book. Like a calling in life, a mission that had not been visible to me, I felt compelled to bring the prairie to life in a positive and constructive fashion, in a way that shared its strengths and beauty, in a format that could be appreciated by readers from all walks of life.

As Walt Whitman and Henry David Thoreau told us long ago, companionship with nature, the mysterious, awe-inspiring out-of-doors, can stimulate a need to look inward. The truth of their words was indeed my reality; the prairie lands, along with an inquisitive nature to begin with, pushed me to consider the whys and wherefores of life within the context of my early surroundings. And throughout my life, whenever difficult questions emerge I find myself drawn to the prairie in a personal quest for answers, insight, and greater self-knowledge. It is there where I find room to breathe.

Now, in considering the sentiments of Whitman and Thoreau, the words of scholars and pundits that are often descriptive, poetic, and deeply inspiring, stirring our souls and imaginations like nothing else, I have to wonder if we haven't depended on their literary, soul-wise talents for too long, clinging to the past like frightened baby birds instead of pushing on—as we must—in a heartfelt search for what is real in today's world. Because only then can we create a truly promising future for the children and grandchildren who will inevitably follow in our footsteps.

For it seems our ideas have grown stale, while our hearts have hardened and our souls have grown weary. I have to believe our complacency would have shocked and saddened the pioneers, left them wondering why our nation has made so little progress in the areas that matter (equality, personal freedom, justice, concern for all human beings, meaningful challenge), especially when so many gave their lives, the lives of their children, in a quest for freedom, personal dignity, and a cherished opportunity to test their own strength. The hardships were innumerable; the illusions were few; the rewards were nearly always intangible. Yet, their path, indeed, their journey, was filled with heart; otherwise, they could never have survived such steep challenges. And, so it is that in our search for inspiration and knowledge, we, too, must gather our courage, moving forward like pioneers, bravely stepping beyond the forceful words and interpretations of the past, as we humbly ask the prairie for more.

This is not an easy task.

The place itself, the prairie and its culture, speaks softly, almost whisperlike at times, so it can be difficult to truly capture its essence. Glorious, yes, splendid and breathtaking as well; but it is also stark, expansive, and surreal. It is all of this and more. To me, to my prairie heart, the lands of South Dakota evoke feelings of pure delight. Untouched and free, the prairie symbolizes the great unknown—past, present, and future all in one, a convincing space knowing no boundaries or limits, no worries or demons: a place where my heart resides.

Yet it is reasonably certain that these open lands, this place, does not effect everyone in precisely the same way. There have been times in my life when I resented the prairie and everything it stood for, everything it seemed to ask of me; and there have been times when I misunderstood its firm grip on my heart and soul. But in finally coming to terms with the land, in being able to articulate its value and its essence, for you, at this point in my life, I realize just how far "we" have come together: the prairie and I.

Like best friends who have been through the good and the bad yet survived, growing ever stronger through the inevitable struggles, disappointments, and challenges life offers, the prairie and I have weathered the storm together, and at long last it has won my heart. It can be difficult to speculate on the feelings of others, however, because many who grow up with the prairie, many who live there now, rarely speak of its impact on their lives—of its curious force and quiet strength, its simple demands and rich rewards.

Like sacred ground, people of the prairie cherish the land quietly, without fanfare or formal proclamation, as the land commands a good deal of reverence and respect, much like the oceans, outer space, or a towering mountain range. Within this "far-removed" context, the urgency and complexities of contemporary life fade, the prairie landscape encouraging contemplation while gently drawing something pure, surprisingly charming, from us, something we did not even suspect was there.

Walt Whitman wrote a prose poem as he crossed the Great Plains in 1879; published in 1882, it appeared in *Speciman Days* and was called "The Prairies and an Undelivered Speech." "But if you care to have a word with me," he wrote, "I should speak it about these very prairies; they impress me most, of all the objective shows I see or have seen on this, my first real visit to the West.

"I wonder indeed if the people of this continental inland West know how much of a first-class art they have in these prairies—how original and all your own—how much of the influences of a character for your future humanity, broad, patriotic, heroic, and new?"

As Whitman correctly senses, the prairie lands have much to offer, yet can be equally difficult to comprehend, absorb, or appreciate with any degree of success or satisfaction; they can frustrate, subdue, and provoke. Decked out in its natural grandeur, safely hidden from the public glare in the heart of South Dakota, the prairie, I know, has tucked itself into a way of life that has grown up around it. Like a happily married couple, the people and the prairie have become one over the years.

It is indeed a good place for our journey to begin.

Because now, as we place our magnifying lens on this place, on these people, tidbits of truth, priceless and pure like morning dew on blades of summer grass, emerge, and it is these charms of the heart, these magical prairie treasures, that offer us new hope.

That offer us all . . . room to breathe.

WHERE
THE
HEART
RESIDES

If there was a road I could not make it out in the faint starlight.
There was nothing but land: not a country at all, but the
material out of which countries are made.

—WILLA CATHER,
My Antonia

ENVISION A WINDOW
TO THE HEART

It is here that we begin our journey into the private, well-preserved folds of the prairie and its culture, starting with the origin and value of an informal philosophy based on the nuances of place, people, and time. Because, in myriad ways, the prairie is a place filled with charming possibilities, a place where the heart resides; and when you take the prairie and its people into your heart and life, no matter where you live, you will begin to sense the quiet strength, the peace and the power, of a landscape that has brought men, women, and children to their knees—deftly, without regard for race, religion, age, stature, education, or gender. In the eyes of the prairie, we are equals, no matter what.

While you may want to mold the finer details of this prairie-wise philosophy to your individual needs, personal preferences, and circumstances, the prairie's essence supersedes and surpasses state lines, city limits, personal and neighborhood cliques.

And fortunately, getting to know the prairie is a function of the heart—an orientation transported without plane, train, or automobile—and prairie wisdom is a set of beliefs that transcend, join, and inspire. So you see, the prairie and its culture are more than a place on a map; even with a small population—in South Dakota there are about 700,000 people in all—there is incredible value in what the area has to offer, there is most definitely, heart. And there is plenty of charm, enough to inspire nations of people the world over.

You need not live there to benefit, nor must you adopt the prairie's teachings hook, line, and sinker; that is truly part of its mystique. Rather, the wisdom of the prairie, like a precious stone, can be carved out in the form of words, pictures, and concepts that reach out and touch the heart—the seat of passion and change, of all that we hold dear.

William A. Quayle wrote in *The Prairie and the Sea*, "You must not be in the prairie; but the prairie must be in you. That alone will do as qualification for biographer of the prairie. . . . He who tells the prairie mystery must wear the prairie in his heart."

As one who wears the prairie in my heart, I am eager to share its mysteries, so that regardless of where you reside, you, too, can carry the prairie, its inspiring messages, in your heart. And should you have an opportunity to visit or even live there one day, so much the better, but as the final chapter points out: come and go. Prairie life is not for everyone, nor should it be; its purpose, as the pages of this book reveal, is much greater.

The prairie's teachings are universally significant and globally intriguing, because, you see, wisdom that is born of the heart can be modified to suit individual proclivities; it can be used to nurture the dreams and desires of people of all ages and walks of life. For love is the great unifier, the ingredient that contains enough passion and power to change lives, inspire us to great heights, move us to tears of joy or great pain, motivate us to examine our beliefs and values or make the compromises of a lifetime.

Whatever your destiny, goals, problems, joys, or challenges, a little prairie wisdom along the way, "a window to the heart," will serve you well.

A DANCE WITH DESTINY

We all have a destiny in life. For me, it was growing up on the prairie—on the plains of central South Dakota. And while I do not remember my first encounter with the land, nor my first impressions, I do recall the open spaces being *all around me*, and I also recall being outside with my grandmother in her yard exploring flowers, heaps of walnuts, and the lily-white blossoms that covered her apple trees in the spring. Somewhere along the way, maybe as a young girl or as a teenager, maybe even later in life, during college when I returned home to see family and friends, to visit my grandmother who was by then in her late eighties, the prairie made its presence known to me. In contrast to what I experienced in Missouri, where I attended Stephens College, the prairie was undeniably different.

The air, often sticky and damp, created a thick haze at times, a musty smell; the sky seemed distant, not as compelling; the rain was intense and frequent; trees seemed to be everywhere, while the winds were often mild, a light breeze, to me. And the winter came and went without being much noticed at all. But above all else, the part that bothered me then, and still does, was that I could never seem to find the sunset or the sunrise, not in the way I remembered seeing them in the open spaces of home. There was too much in the way, too much that came between me and the sky. I felt cut off from the beautiful surroundings I had known, and taken for granted during my youth, by silent barriers.

Everything seemed watered down—less vibrant and intense, not magnetic or thought provoking, less magical in its ability to comfort and inspire, to lift my spirits with images of the great unknown. I was indeed a "stranger in a strange land," as Thomas Wolfe put it in *Look Homeward,*

Angel, and as reflected in the book title, *Stranger in a Strange Land*, a science fiction story written by Robert Heinlein. While some would not have taken note of the geographical and societal differences to the extent I did, for me it was a strong signal to dig deeper, to figure out who I was in relation to this new land, this place, *not of the prairie*, that seemed to want to overshadow and hide the things I had grown to love.

My search "to understand" followed me: no matter where I lived, no matter what I did, refusing to be ignored, refusing to let me rest for long. But in my quest for answers, in my willingness to ask tough questions that tease and taunt us like merciless riddles, I learned to live with ambiguity; I also learned to value the process, the ongoing search for truth and understanding that had come to define my life.

The prairie had presented me with a puzzle of life-size proportion, and in my attempt to solve it over the years, at times letting the pieces sit idle for a while, just simmering in my mind, something has pulled me back to it time and time again. And now, having written this book to finally complete the puzzle, I assume nothing, knowing the prairie, the ideas it has forced me to consider, probably has more tricks up its sleeve.

So I take this brief interlude in a life's journey to bring to light useful prairie teachings acquired over a lifetime, ideas and concepts worth sharing, because the message of the prairie is really quite cosmopolitan, and at the turn of the century especially beneficial. As we pause to consider those who preceded us, our history as a people and as a nation, indeed, where we are headed, it is only natural to glance backward and inward; it is only wise to search our heart and soul for answers. Thus, it is from this perspective that we begin our journey inward, because to become prairie wise you must be willing to get to know yourself better each day; you must be concerned about emotional, intellectual, and spiritual survival in today's somewhat wearisome world.

Because, as you have probably gathered by now, prairie wisdom is about learning to look, really look, at life in a way that spotlights the inconsequential, peers under and below the shiny, glittery surface of things, delves into the dusty corners and invisible crevices of life in an effort to understand the truth of the matter, indeed, the heart of the matter.

There is plenty of time for that on the prairie—fewer people, fewer distractions—so it is naturally a place that invites questions and serious contemplation about the things in life that truly matter: self-discovery, hope, kind deeds, integrity, love, courage and conviction, and whatever else is at the top of your list.

With equal fervor, the land, plain and understated, downplays materialism, pretentious ways, and false judgments that fail to honor the humanness in us all.

As William Least Heat-Moon explains in *PrairyErth (A Deep Map) An Epic History of the Tallgrass Prairie County*, a monumental book about the prairie lands of Chase County, Kansas: "I came to understand that the prairies are nothing but grass as the sea is nothing but water, that most prairie life is within the place: under the stems, below the turf, beneath the stones. The prairie is not a topography that shows its all but rather a vastly exposed place of concealment . . . where the splendid lies within the plain cover."

That is not to say that the prairie is a perfect place, nor are its inhabitants. But without a doubt, it is a different kind of place, one that does not reveal its treasures easily, yet one that can draw out the best in you, forcing you to go beyond absolutes and black-and-white thinking—superficial distinctions that alienate and divide. And even though the state's history is speckled, like a multicolored Easter egg, with good and bad, holy and evil, birth and death, it is also rich and powerful, offering an incredible opportunity to sort through the complexities and contradictions of life. Providing a mesmerizing framework for meaningful observation, for the development of a philosophy of life that is informal and curiously commonsensical, and, even now, as it evolves, as the prairie's wisdom seeps into my heart, peers around the corner, when I least expect it, I sense my inability to capture it "all."

Yet forge ahead we must; as wisdom, in any tradition, by any other name, is far from an exact science, and in sharing my experience and understanding of these distant lands, a deep honor that has brought me to tears on numerous pages, it is my primary hope that each of you who read this book will derive something unique from the prairie's essence: insights, novel ways in which to apply the ideas and observations tucked inside this charming, unusually compelling, book. We are in this journey together, and each of you will have something worthwhile to contribute along the way.

I am equally certain that as you traverse the prairie lands in the year 2000 and beyond you will be inspired to consider what "used to be" and "what is" from a new vantage point. Because the past lives on in our hearts, and as we reconnect with parts of ourselves that are lost or misplaced, ideas previously discarded or tossed aside will strike a chord. A bit like hearing from an old friend, your eyes will light up, your mind will buzz with happy thoughts and memories, your heart will eagerly reach out for more. We "know" more than we think we know, a good deal of which we have simply forgotten.

Luckily, for all of us, the prairie, the place and its people, has not changed much. Still there, patiently waiting for our return, and now, at the turn of the century, what a perfect time to rekindle the warm fires of old, what a grand time to reconsider the wisdom that already resides within our hearts . . . maybe dust covered or slightly misshapen, but quietly waiting for our return like the distant prairie lands.

In using this book as your guide, you will find bits and pieces of information tied together, bundled up like a welcome Sunday newspaper with something for everyone: humor, history, fascinating connections; ideas revisited, renewed, updated, or clarified; colorful quotes from experts and students of the prairie; wise and wonderful sayings based on nature and life experience; descriptive passages that paint a vivid picture of the prairie landscape; photographs that impart a lasting image.

As Thoreau wisely noted in his journal entry for December 31, 1841: "In society you will not find health, but in nature. You must converse much with the fields and woods if you would imbibe such health into your mind and spirit as you covet for your body."

So, with the pioneer spirit in our hearts, let us push onward, let us consider the intricacies of place.

PRAIRIE DIMENSIONS

The prairie lands I have experienced most intimately are situated in central South Dakota, in the very heart of the prairie, so let us get our bearings by considering the state as a whole. On a map, South Dakota looks square, basic, and deceptively consistent, but the state has two distinct sections: East River and West River. The split designations have been around as far back as anyone can recall, yet there is nothing more than friendly rivalry between the two sides. The state is not large enough to survive too much inner turmoil. That, and a good deal of old-fashioned pride, keeps South Dakotans basically unified.

Likewise, each side of the state has its share of tiny, pebblelike communities that are nothing more than a fleck of dust on the planet's surface.

What you will find in these small towns is simple: a few trees, probably cottonwoods; a miniature grocery store of six to ten rows; an old gas station; the corner post office; and a few residential streets attached at the sides or in the back, much like an afterthought. Places like Ipswich, Mud Butte, Epiphany, Isabel, Glad Valley, Badger, Hub City, Ralph, Buffalo Gap, Olivet, Fedora, and Crow Lake dot the South Dakota horizon along with towns like Red Elm, Prairie City, Long Lake, and Bonesteel. A mesmerizing mix of names that gently paws at the imagination, and like a rake against grass and leaves in the fall of the year, just hearing the names of these small, unpretentious towns stirs the soul.

What is there? What is behind the town's name, if anything? What are the people like and what in heaven's name do they do? Why are they there and what do they believe?

The names are colorful, somehow majestic in their simplicity, and as a matter of geographic reference, these towns are often situated smack dab in the middle of the prairie, nearly always within a stone's throw of open grassland.

From that point on, South Dakota towns come in all shapes and sizes, culminating with Sioux Falls, the state's largest city. With a population of more than 100,000 people, it is located in the southeastern corner of the state; Rapid City, a West River community, is the state's second-largest city. Located in southwestern South Dakota, Rapid is a lovely mountain town that connects to the Black Hills and is only a few miles from Mount Rushmore. This is the touristy part of the state.

With Crazy Horse—the world's largest sculpture at 563 feet high, 641 feet long, and supervised by sculptor Korczak Ziolkowski until his death in 1982—forming on Thunderhead Mountain (near Custer, South Dakota), along with the revitalization of Deadwood, a mining town made famous during the gold rush of 1876, the western part of the state is destined to grow in popularity and population.

The central part of the state is home to the Oahe Dam—one of the world's largest earth-rolled dams—the state capital, numerous Canadian geese that winter on Capitol Lake (it is warmed by an artesian well), and countless pheasant and deer. Pierre is the community that holds it all together, and that is where I grew up in the late fifties and early sixties; a beautiful river town of about 13,000 people, the area is a fishing and hunting haven for many. Hunters fly in from all over the country for the annual Governor's Hunt, a highly publicized pheasant hunt held each fall. A good guide service, for hunting or fishing, can do quite well. Lodges are springing up wherever wildlife abound, from primitive to elaborate, with prices for a "gun" tapping out at around $2000 for a three-day weekend. Try www.uplandriver.com to take a peek at one!

With the beautiful Missouri River running along the town's southern boundary, it is commonplace to own a boat. Some kind of boat, any kind of boat, really. Known as the walleye capital of the world, fishing is a popular pastime, and tournaments of national distinction draw fishermen from all across the United States; the weigh-in ceremonies are well attended. And each spring, when fishing is at its finest, the sparkling river waters, especially in the early morning hours, are dotted with boats of all sizes and shapes. For some, fishing is serious business; for others, it is a pleasant time to relax and contemplate life. For me, it was a bit of both. Not learning how to fish until I was in my late thirties, I remember well my dislike of worms, of having to actually touch one if I were to have the right kind of bait on the end of my line. Minnows weren't a problem, however, so when walleyes were biting on jigs and minnows, those were better days.

And the thrill of catching my first fish: not a large one, but a walleye nonetheless, the small white tip on the end of the tail, the memorable eyes, making the identity clear; it was an exciting moment, one that never seemed to grow old—even on a good day when the fish were biting no matter how poor the fisherman or fisherwoman. I soon learned to watch the river for clues; the "walleye chop," when the wind causes the water to roll and toss in easy, lilting waves, is one of them. It is then that you should drop everything and go fishing because, under these conditions, the movement of your boat is camouflaged from the elusive walleye.

Another popular way to fish for walleye is to pull plugs (poles baited with a "wally diver" perhaps and cast out the back of the boat as it trolls down the river at a steady clip); this, I don't think I have mastered, but plan to give it another try someday.

Interestingly, however, when I tell people I grew up in South Dakota, near sparkling water and windswept prairie, cradled by the maternal lands and naively thinking this was the way everyone lived, their questions are often predictable and slightly entertaining. "Is there anything to do up there?" they ask with a sudden frown, or "Does everyone drive a pickup truck?" Or maybe he'll say "I bet that's a good place to get a pair of cowboy boots, maybe a cowboy hat?" Then, with a funny twist of her head, "It really snows up there, doesn't it?" Yet one question always predominates: "Do you pronounce Pierre, Peer or peeair?" And so it goes, until I wonder why no one ever asks a good question, one that would force me to stop and think for at least a minute or two. (For those who are curious, "Pierre" is pronounced *peer*. Technically, since the town's origins are French, the correct pronunciation is *Peeair*, but Dakotans are a stubborn bunch, preferring to say "peer" nonetheless.)

A discussion of South Dakota would not be complete without touching on the area's notorious climate. Famous for its extremes, it is a toss-up as to which is worse, winter or summer, because both seasons can be intense, ranging from dreadfully hot, dry summers to bitterly cold winters. On the whole, prairie winters are long-lived, featuring blowing snow, steep drifts, below-zero temperatures—all of which make going out unappealing, if not impossible. I remember plenty of blizzards when a look outside revealed nothing more than a blinding white blur, and even though we lived in town, where the wind was slightly less free, I still couldn't see across the street.

The ferocious wind, sometimes fickle and unnerving, is part and parcel of life on the prairie; much has been written about prairie winds, the one "constant" during all four seasons. Windmills, in all semblances of repair, still dot the horizon.

As Kathleen Norris has noted in *Dakota*, "Many mornings, when the wind has come up during the night, the trees around my house thunder like high surf that swells and ebbs without cease. . . . The wind can be a welcome companion on a hot day, but even die-hard Dakotans grow tired when the sky howls and roars at forty miles an hour for a day or more." Wileta Welty Hawkins, a long-time resident now eighty-nine, put it like this: "When I moved to South Dakota, I thought I would die! No trees. And the wind!" No doubt, it is a force to be reckoned with, but nature reigns supreme on the prairie, the wind merely the persistent messenger. So while it is ridiculed by outsiders and insiders alike, most people tolerate the wind with a certain amount of prairie aplomb: It is there for a reason.

Evenings begin to cool off by mid-August, and in the summer the days are incredibly long. There is nothing quite like a summer evening on the prairie—quiet and mystical, the stillness and the wanning light can practically give me goose bumps. But there are also plenty of raging thunderstorms, some rather nasty, in fact, but rain, in general, is typically scarce, so when it finally comes down, even as a delicate sprinkle, there is just cause for celebration. Hail, however, is cause for concern. Often dropping from the sky with the force of a high-speed drill and very little warning, for farmers hail usually spells trouble, if not a big loss.

Yet spring, as a rule, can be a glorious time, especially when there is at least *some* rain associated with it. That is when the prairie comes to life with free-flowing wildflowers; sometimes tiny and timid in appearance, but often vibrant in color, prairie flowers make their quiet and dependable debut at a time when all of nature seems to be proudly announcing its winter survival. On the prairie that is not something to be taken lightly.

Winter survival is an accomplishment, you see, and its spirit, vivid and real on the prairie, is somehow contagious: a time to share in nature's joyful resurgence, to greet another growing season with a grateful and expectant heart.

Fall can be a slightly different story, however. The season can come early on the prairie and is best described as a mixture of lingering summer days, early winter days, and a few somewhere in-between. Not long ago, a Halloween snowfall caught plenty of prairie dwellers by surprise. Yet as a general observation, autumn's arrival is greeted with mixed feelings: the blistering-hot days of summer are over, but the cold winter snow will soon fly again.

When I think of the prairie in the fall, fields of gigantic drooping sunflowers come to mind, along with images of massive combines gently roving the countryside against a blazing red-orange sunset. Add to that a wonderful earthy smell; rich and full, it is a stout mix of grain, prairie dust, and late-blooming flowers like golden chrysanthemums and burnt-orange marigolds. A powerful smell that fills the senses and stirs the soul with festive feelings of completeness, a warm prairie autumn can be a real treasure, one to hold in your heart as an ongoing source of inspiration and joy.

THE PRAIRIE AND ITS PEOPLE

So who are these people, the people who, out of choice or circumstance, live in the middle of nowhere? Are they as mysterious as the place, or over time have they simply become one with the land? Do they love feeling isolated from the world, insulated from "city problems," or do they sometimes sense they are missing out on all the excitement? Curiously enough, all of the above are true.

The people of South Dakota are surprisingly diverse in their viewpoints, more than you may expect; individually, they are as unique as any other population. There are, of course, certain tendencies and general patterns that effectively supersede the differences, perceived or factual. Like the East River/West River debate that rages on as a matter of course, many of the differences among the people are superficial ones. As a "collective," there is a common bond that creates a spirit of unity, strength, and cohesion, because when it comes right down to it, people of the prairie share many beliefs and values, and when the chips are down, they rally around each other like family members.

A measure of loyalty comes with time, shared experience, and mutual dependence, and you can find a good number of old-timers who would not move if their lives depended on it. The area gets its share of new arrivals, too. Some come to escape city life, others are returning to their roots; some wind up there because of a spouse or a job. Depending on the situation, transitions are easy for some, while others endure tedious months of "culture shock."

Those who return to the area after a prolonged absence usually marvel at how little things have changed during the past five, ten, or even twenty years.

Change does occur, and the latest conveniences eventually arrive, but only in due time and not because there is any significant demand for either one. Anything that represents change, things and ideas considered new, are sprinkled on top of the old very lightly and usually only as an afterthought, never as the main dish: There is too much fondness and genuine appreciation for what is already there.

Many of the prairie's people are in love with a way of life that has existed for a long time; it is as if they sense their uniqueness, the very specialness of the area. Yet such sentiments are rarely discussed, not openly anyway. Prairie residents tend to be modest, quiet, and relatively private. Some are afraid that too much talk might be detrimental to their lifestyle, which, for many, is a prairie paradise; many simply prefer that outsiders admire their state from a considerable distance.

That is not to say that South Dakotans are an inhospitable bunch. The majority of them simply value what they have, some actually consider themselves spoiled, and most would like to avoid problems of the big-city variety. So, in many ways, parts of the state are in a preservation mode, which often leaves people feeling threatened by outside influences. Yet therein lies an economic and real-world dilemma: Nothing stands still forever.

On some level, within any system or organization, there must be change and growth because basic survival depends on it, but in some areas there is a deep reluctance to change, a clear resistance to new ideas and ways of doing things. Prairie dwellers, like everyone else, read the newspapers, watch television, travel, and listen to the radio. They know what it is like "out there."

And while some of it may look enticing and sound appealing, for the most part these people, young and old alike, favor the status quo. Living on the prairie is relatively safe, comfortable, and reliable, and while certain career opportunities are not readily available, and from a strictly economic perspective most salaries are not impressive, many residents believe these "facts of life" are a necessary trade-off, one they are willing to make.

A general lack of resources around the state is simply accepted as part of the area's heritage, and even though residents may complain about it now and then most are wise enough to know that limited financial resources does not translate to a spiritual or intellectual deficiency. In fact, materialistic limitations may be responsible for the state's special qualities, the ones money can't buy or simulate. That very dynamic is in keeping with Thoreau's thinking. "Do not trouble yourself much," he says, "to get new things, whether new clothes or new friends. . . . Superfluous wealth can buy superfluities only. Money is not required to buy one necessary of the soul." If right then, he is even more accurate today. We see the resurgence of his thinking all around: books on caring for the soul, articles about doing with less to find true happiness, movies that feature a return to heart and soul, an amazing variety of self-help tapes telling us to throw off financial concerns in exchange for peace of mind and spiritual growth.

Yet this is not new thinking on the prairie; this is a way of life. Growing up there, as part of my particular and individual dance with destiny, I learned at a fairly young age to view materialistic gains with a cautious and skeptical eye. Plenty of people seemed content, joyous, and complete with the simple things in life, and those with significantly greater resources, the minority, no doubt, didn't seem any happier. My imagination perhaps, but now, as I look around me, to consider the people

I have known over the years in different states and circumstances, it is quite clear to me that material wealth is no guarantee of anything.

Life is, and always has been, more complex.

Character comes in all sizes, shapes, and colors. Happiness comes from within. And peace of mind, that rare and glorious commodity, is something each of us, regardless of external circumstances, must work at achieving and maintaining each day.

PRAIRIE WISE

In sum, this was my framework, my unique perspective on life, when I left the safe confines of the prairie. Fortunately, I took with me a strong sense of identity, plenty of self-respect, and a quiet sort of confidence nurtured by my time on the prairie, by my experience of its culture, by my quiet companionship with the land. More important, perhaps, I had learned to question the obvious, to look below the surface of any situation for a deeper truth, a more meaningful reality.

I firmly believe that if we take the time to look, to perceive, and to care, discovery is always within our grasp. Most things are not what they seem—more or less maybe, yet different from what superficial observation suggests. Perhaps this is why I did my graduate work in sociology. Intrigued by prairie life, the modern-day version included, ever since I ventured out into the world as a young college student, I felt well prepared to study the "science of society." I had learned firsthand that a seemingly poor state was, in many ways, rich because of its intrinsic value, because it is a place where the heart resides, and I had already discovered parts of myself, at a relatively young age, that, had circumstances been much different, would have been difficult to find at any age.

Sure, I had heard about hard times, about the trials and tribulations of the pioneers, but I had also caught wind of enchanting survival stories, plenty of them; I saw a few of them firsthand. When problems looked insurmountable, people kept going, radiating a "can do" spirit that helped them prevail no matter how bad things actually got. And there was such pride in accomplishment; I saw that, too.

From a great crop to a new baby or a bountiful garden, life itself seemed to be enough, and being without a new car, a new anything, was not automatic cause for alarm or dismay. Of course I also learned that people of the land were sometimes looked down on by those who did not understand or appreciate the inherent richness of their ways: the prairie view. I knew the term "country hicks." But no, I soon decided, not true, just warm, down-to-earth country people with heart—people who take things one day at a time and usually "with a grain of salt."

The old-timers have seen too much, experienced too much to worry about sophisticated ways, and a good number of them have inherited a strong, independent spirit. As one longtime resident says, "I ignore people who try to boss me; I believe in equality and think I should have my own say-so." With a noticeable twinkle in her eye, Wileta Hawkins, so named after her father, William, also advises people "to make the best of things, no matter what."

So now, my appreciation for the prairie—its flavor, people, and culture—is strong and clear. And while there have been times in my life (like now) when I lived elsewhere, times when I felt closed in and closed off by the prairie to the point of unhappiness, as I ponder the ways of the world I am increasingly grateful for the tremendous diamond-in-the-rough-opportunity I had in growing up there, a place that may be closer to heaven than most people care to imagine.

As I realize now, growing up prairie wise was a special chance to learn about life on a fundamental level by offering a rare look at what is and is not important, something that normally takes a lifetime to figure out. Thus, the prairie spirit runs deep in my heart and soul; I carry it with me no matter where I go, no matter who I meet or what I do.

Especially useful in today's society, with its plenitude of distractions, multitude of ways to avoid and hide from reality, legion of false definitions of success built into a fast-paced society to the point where values and priorities have been distorted, twisted, and abolished, where many have simply given up, and where many are looking for an easy way out, a shortcut through life offering nothing but bliss and good times, I cherish the lessons of land, sky, and wide-open space. Because, oddly enough, with all we have created as a society, genuine happiness seems more elusive than ever; just when we believe we have found *it*, we begin to complain as our discovery begins to feel strange, empty, or curiously nondescript. Slowly slipping through our fingers. But still, the mindless chase goes on, happiness being falsely equated with comfort, status, and possessions when such distinctions serve to block our human view, keeping us lost and floundering. Effectively, at bay, from more meaningful pursuits.

When one new car doesn't work, buy another one. When the latest house doesn't work, get a bigger one on a bigger lot. And when the newest, most fashionable clothes don't work either, try a better watch, a big-screen television, or maybe a bigger swimming pool.

That is not to say it is wrong to desire or accumulate objects that can bring us pleasure, but as the unencumbered prairie lands seem to point out, when you expect these things to create and sustain happiness, disappointment will ultimately follow. Life, in all its many dimensions, is so much more. And genuine happiness, like everything else in life, must be based on knowledge of self, a willingness to endure difficult times, an ongoing commitment to what is "real."

As Frances Nickel Jones, age 104 in 1999, states: "I guess working that hard must have agreed with me."

Frances, a homesteader near the Bad River area of west-central South Dakota in the early 1900s with her husband, Louis, experienced more hard times than she sometimes cares to remember, but very little, even now, gets her down. For starters, when Louis died in 1928, she did not give up. She and her two young sons hitched up the horses to go to church; chopped river ice for the cattle; cut and hauled enough river-bottom wood to last an entire winter; raised turkeys and shipped them off to Chicago by rail; survived dust, grasshoppers, and plenty of prairie rattlers.

Yet despite it all, Frances is a happy and spirited woman. Her eyes twinkle; she listens to what others have to say with interest and concern; she often has something insightful to say; and, amazingly enough, Frances didn't bother to sell her house and move into a group living situation until she turned 100. A local celebrity due to her age and joyous nature, Frances Jones, her life and her personality, is a strong manifestation of the prairie spirit. Her life was tough but, like the prairie, she survived. And Frances is indeed prairie wise.

She agrees that the easy life is little more than a vacuum, a big, black hole that neither sustains nor rewards, so she does not understand why people are so soft these days.

A testament to the prairie, of all it offers and teaches, Frances is magical in inspiration, and her happy spirit will undoubtedly outlive us all. Like the majestic prairie lands, she seems to want to say: *Wake up! There is more to life than you think.* But first there must be the time and the willingness to really dig into life instead of skimming along the surface with unfocused busyness.

So now, as we consider a perspective that results in doing more of what counts, less of what causes you to lose your way, you will be ever closer to envisioning a road map to the heart. A clear destination, one to propel you forward with the stalwart intentions of a pioneer in a covered wagon, is the first step to discovering, for yourself, the charms of the heart—magical prairie treasures for a more hopeful world.

Why should we live with such hurry and waste of life?
We are determined to be starved before we are hungry.

—HENRY DAVID THOREAU,
Walden

DISCOVER
YOUR TRUTH

There is a prairie antidote to the frenetic pace, the maddening pressures, of everyday life: Practice and perfect the fine art of doing nothing. Build it into your day, your way of life, your game plan for success, and do not wait until you are unable to do anything—an entirely different situation. Unless you have carved out an exceptional life for yourself, you are probably burning the candle at both ends, moving at the speed of light, dancing as fast as you can. This is a common predicament, one that has plagued mankind for decades, and while we all wish for greater balance in our lives, rarely are we able to live up to our own expectations and seldom do our most admirable intentions see us through.

You must think in terms of practice: Change comes gradually and only with long-term commitment, resistance is guaranteed. Yet even under the best of conditions, you may be truly incapable of doing less, so doing nothing is next to incomprehensible. When you try to settle down or calm down, your mind and body will not let you rest; your family and friends will not let you be; your restless soul will not let you tarry, even pause to enjoy your surroundings—the people or the place. It is understandable, of course.

Programmed from birth by society, workplaces, and those you love to act and react, perform, produce, prod, push, and pull, you are simply falling in line with the explicit and implicit desires of those around you.

The prairie offers an enlightened alternative, one that teaches something powerful and true: Doing less paves the way for doing more. This message, a highly suitable one for our harried times, comes through loud and clear on a visual level. A thoughtful survey of the land reveals a place, *a space*, basking in a nearly timeless state, as if suspended in some sort of magical potion.

Vast stretches of flat land, gently rolling hills with slopes and curves of seemingly artistic origin, wide-brimmed sunsets, wildlife that scurry around like self-important diplomats, lazy skies extending high and long above the fray—above our daily plodding—dusty gravel roads without beginning or end: Try to picture it. Let the word "hurry" disintegrate into a nameless blur. The message is obvious: Hectic schedules, a hurry-up, do-it-now mentality, cannot compare or compete with the persistent beauty and quiet strength of the prairie. As we scramble about each day, dashing here, dashing there, the land does the opposite, and without a word speaks to our souls, touches our hearts, and reaches out, like a laser, to connect with our finer, more discriminating sides.

In the overall scheme of things, our best efforts to stand out above the crowd can only be seen as less than monumental in comparison to the elegance and stature of undisturbed land that is remarkably free of man-made artifacts. Still, in an attempt to make our mark, to get everything done, we get caught up in a vicious cycle of do, do, do, hoping the end result will somehow justify the means. For you, it might.

For others, a continual round of "going and doing" has created a mindless, circular motion that rarely, if ever, ceases despite feelings of fatigue, sadness, or incredible stress. With enough repetition, constant activity—for the sake of activity alone—can begin to feel natural or even necessary, yet unexamined busyness is a clear road to nowhere, one that results in doing less instead of more.

By the time we figure this out, however, the clock may have wound down, and only belatedly do we realize how we failed to stop, look, and listen—when we had the chance, when the time was ours in the first place—how we failed to prioritize *after* consulting our hearts. Unfortunately, many falsely assume that being busy is inherently important, while doing nothing on purpose is the equivalent of being lazy, dull, worthless, or depraved. Not so.

Now, that is not to say that those who live on the prairie believe in doing nothing to the exclusion of pursuits that really do matter, nor am I suggesting it as a way of life no matter where you live. Yet in a remote place like central South Dakota, and elsewhere where the prairie scene dominates, there is a general awareness that the human body, and indeed the spirit, need time, permission, and encouragement to do less.

Because, curiously enough, time to do less often results in something more: time to recharge and regroup; time to stay in touch with feelings, values, beliefs, and, of course, people; time to let events unfold naturally, at their own unique pace; time to do things that support your dreams so you may grow old gracefully, knowing few stones were left unturned.

In a place where connections to others run deep, where everyone knows everyone, it takes a considerable amount of "down time" to nurture such relationships. Growing up on the prairie, I grew accustomed to friendly exchanges that were casual and comfortable, and while fortuitous encounters of the small-town variety may seem insignificant, they actually help form the fabric of daily life on the prairie—sustaining and building, creating a reality that is neither contrived nor high pressure.

When your day is jammed full of must-do, can't-wait items, there isn't time for casual exchanges; there is little opportunity for the unexpected, unplanned, spur-of-the-moment cup of coffee with an old friend, the walk to the park with your son or daughter or spouse. Still, these are activities that contribute to a way of life that promotes the importance, the fundamental value, of the human connection: without fail, without exception, without excuse.

On the prairie that is why it is considered important to go fishing, take a walk, enjoy a spectacular sunset, help a neighbor with some badly needed house repairs, plan a surprise birthday party for an aging (and unsuspecting) relative. Prairie picnics are also a priority, along with "stopping in for coffee." And card parties, usually whist or gin rummy, are a dependable social highlight for people of all ages.

While such activities are clearly not the equivalent of doing nothing, time must be available for such pursuits on an "as needed" basis; it should also be given freely, shared without resentment, keeping score, or feelings of regret. When this happens, as it so often does on the prairie, there is a wonderful flow, a gentle rhythm to each day, a dynamic that allows events to unfold naturally in an unpredictably comfortable manner; a strong sense of give and take, increasingly difficult to find in our overly competitive, urgent world, fuels the fire. And within this context, much is to be gained—for one thing, a lifestyle that supports people! While that may sound strange or simplistic, consider the dehumanizing events of your day or week. Is that how you *want* to live? And what are we doing to ourselves—now and over the long run?

But, you ask, how can "doing nothing" be considered an art form? Isn't it just a matter of crossing off the less important items from a lengthy list? Yes and no.

Successfully doing nothing is an actual art form because it requires that you dig in, study your lifestyle, reconsider priorities, consult your heart and soul, elevate your mind, discipline your well-worn habits, adopt new and novel ways of thinking, contain your weaknesses. Moreover, adopting a "do less to do more" orientation will challenge you because it sounds deceptively simple and easy when it will actually require active decision making. It will push you to make difficult choices; it will yank at your guilt strings; it may cause you to feel silly and inept; it may cause your friends, families, and neighbors to *wonder* about you.

Then, of course, there is boredom to deal with, hyperactive impulses, irritability brought on by self-imposed restraint, and frustration from not seeing the immediate benefit or value of doing less. We live in a world of instant gratification, which implies action, speed, and results.

So, indeed, doing nothing is an art form that requires practice and patience. And as for crossing items off a list, you already know how long that tactic lasts—maybe a day or two.

Ultimately, if you are to use this well-known aspect of prairie wisdom in your life, you will need an open mind, a considerable amount of thought and imagination, a determined attitude. Like so many times in life, it may require a leap of faith.

For encouragement, remind yourself that the less you do, the more you will do: of what counts; of what makes you feel alive and growing; of what helps you become a fully realized human being. For you see, *more than anything*, successfully doing less is a mind-set, an adventure, and a commitment, all of which requires a stout heart and a willingness to take a stand.

A NEW IMAGE

If you live in a city where the pace is truly relentless, or if the whole idea of doing less, and thereby more, sounds remote and abstract, something you cannot quite put your arms around, take heart. While the demands of contemporary society can and do take their toll, often causing the most "together" individual to feel overwhelmed, confused, or frustrated, you can create a new, improved image—a more rewarding lifestyle, a happier spirit.

If the hectic pace feels comfortable for you, if you manage to keep all the right balls in the air, if you do not feel that stress is a major problem in your life, that's fine, too, but realistically, over the long term, a grueling, never-stop lifestyle will catch up with you. So even if you are that unique someone who claims to feel no excessive pressure from the complexities of life, it is important to consider what your lifestyle choices will result in down the road. Creating a life is a bit like designing a magnificent sculpture in your particular image, and good or bad, polished, lopsided, or incomplete, it is your image. For a comparative reference point, consider the prairie's image for a moment. Is it one to emulate? One to cherish, to absorb, and to protect?

Walt Whitman described the prairie like this: unbounded, unconfined, combining the real and the ideal, as beautiful as dreams. That is quite an image. And if the prairie lands are indeed beautiful, then Thomas Moore, the author of *Care of the Soul*, would surely approve of their influence and image as well.

As he points out, "The soul is nurtured by beauty." And "What food is to the body, arresting, complex, and pleasing images are to the soul." Moore goes on, "If we lack beauty in our lives, we will probably suffer familiar disturbances in the soul—depression, paranoia, meaninglessness, and addiction. The soul craves beauty. . . ."

The key, however, is his definition of beauty; if you follow his thinking, the prairie view would top your list. "For the soul, then, beauty is not defined as pleasantness of form but rather as the quality in things that invites absorption and contemplation." He suggests that content and form should be arresting and ". . . lure the heart into profound imagination."

The prairie, known for its magnetic pull, its harmonic overtones, sounds like good food for the soul.

COMING FULL CIRCLE

The settlers, the pioneers, traveled to the prairie more than 100 years ago; indeed, it was a time of exploration and expansion, the prairie lands providing ample opportunity for both. And, so it is in the year 2000 and beyond; only now, our nation has come full circle. In the interim, we have learned that less is more, precisely what the prairie implies and offers; so now we return to these lands through the pages of a small book instead of as pioneers in a covered wagon seeking many of the same things: inspiration and spiritual awakening, a new start, an opportunity to rediscover our potential as a nation—to reclaim the heart of our nation—a chance to put the heart back in our lives. Clearly, the time is right.

As we greet and then surpass the year 2000, a time for reflection, it is important that we journey back to these distant and isolated lands to honor and preserve the prairie culture, to rediscover its truths, to unearth its full bounty. Fortunately, this book offers a unique opportunity to revisit, as a pioneer of the twenty-first century, the unassuming place that became "home" to many of our forefathers—this place where the heart resides.

Based solely on the grandeur of nature and simple, soulful ways, the prairie's wisdom is profoundly emotional, intelligent, and life-enhancing; so even if you never get a chance to experience this place firsthand, to study its splendid texture over time, prairie wisdom, when defined and clarified in contemporary terms, can become part of your life, too.

It is simply part of its charm.

DISCOVER YOUR TRUTH

Once you allow more "open space" into your schedule, and indeed, into your life, you will be one step closer to finding your way back to your heart, *to your truth*, and one step farther away from the short-sighted, self-serving ways that seem to predominate in modern-day society. And while the first step may indeed be the hardest, to prevail is the prairie way, to forge on is the pioneer spirit. Is it alive within you?

These are the gardens of the desert, these
The unshorn fields, boundless and beautiful,
For which the speech of England has no name—
The prairies.

—WILLIAM CULLEN BRYANT,
The Prairies

෨

BUILD A BRIDGE
TO YOURSELF

You have an internal clock—one that says slow down, move on, take your time—but how often do you consult it, how often do you quickly dismiss it? How often do you run right over it in a vain, misguided attempt to stay in control of, reasonably on top of, your almighty schedule? Nearly all the time you may be thinking.

Fortunately, there is still something called prairie time. If you visit there, you will notice it right away; if you are a resident, you are most likely in tune with it and would not trade it for crates of gold, barrels of oil, a lifetime supply of apple pie or chocolate cake. Not now, not ever. On the prairie, time is not rushed or based on impatient attitudes. Rather, prairie time is sweetly balanced, rhythmical, and flexible; as we have already seen, it even allows for the unexpected.

Like a godsend, prairie time is based on natural, internal states, deep human longings too readily ignored and denied in a world that wants everything yesterday and waits for no one.

Yet once you understand the prairie's rhythm, its place in our world, another commonsense tenet of prairie wisdom is unearthed: Build a bridge to yourself. Its importance is obvious. When you are out of step with your private rhythm, you are, in sum, out of step with yourself, and you are most assuredly out of step with the cosmos.

Still, you may push on, relentless in your pursuits, short-sighted in your vision, cut off from the vitality of your spirit. If this is the case, is it any wonder that your activities lack heart—at work, at home, at play? Or any wonder that, as a whole, the people of our nation seem disillusioned, exhausted, and forlorn? Out of deep frustration, more than anything else, we question everything from the basic values that made this country great to the fundamental need to properly care for our emotional and spiritual needs in a world that says: *There is no time.*

To heal ourselves, our nation, and our world, we must have enough courage to consider where we have been and where we are going. More than anything, we must build a better bridge to ourselves so we do not begin to resemble pea-brained robots. Slowing down to savor the absolute richness of life, the wondrous things happening all around us, will help restore our hearts; it will open the door to what is locked inside each of us. It will help us find new solutions to problems of old.

The first step is to consult yourself, your well of internal wisdom; and, by the way, you do not have to be old and gray to possess wisdom. Too often discounted as a meaningless hunch, inklings or ideas that quietly bubble to the surface at unpredictable times or come in sudden waves of knowledge and insight may be tidbits of wisdom seeking expression. Unfortunately, you may decide to ignore such thoughts and feelings, as wisdom can be confused with nonconformity.

Then, sadly, some of your more useful and unique insights are not given due credit even though true wisdom, a revelation that may not be explainable in concrete, rational terms, knows no rules or boundaries. Perhaps that is why some skeptics treat "wisdom" with such suspicion and outright contempt.

It occurs to me, however, that since the heart is inherently wise and knowing, could it be, *could it be*, that in shutting down our hearts to protect ourselves from pain, in closing ourselves off from the world and all its many problems, we are unintentionally blocking the natural flow of wisdom from entering and therefore, from bettering, our lives? Do heart and wisdom go hand in hand? And how could they not?

To take advantage of the wisdom your heart possesses, however, you need to consult your heart more often—you need to be in touch with yourself on an ongoing basis.

Let's return to the idea of an inner clock, to something called prairie time.

While prairie settlers often complained of loneliness, of long, dreary days filled with silence, worry, and sorrow, when they recorded their memoirs as Walker Wyman did for Bruce Siberts in *Nothing but Prairie and Sky: Life on the Dakota Range in the Early Days*, most are eager to share their stories, remembering the very "sweetness" of their lives.

Siberts was seventy-seven when he contacted Wyman to help him put his thoughts and recollections together, and during the five years that followed, between 1945 and 1950, he produced over 900 pages in longhand; by then he was eighty-two. And although he died in 1952, two years before his book was published, Siberts would have treasured the end product, a charming and illuminating memoir of his life on the prairie from 1890 to 1906, as edited and prepared by a Wisconsin State University professor of history.

Homesteading near Plum Creek, a few miles west of Pierre, South Dakota, in an area commonly known as West River country, Siberts lived as a bachelor in a crude shack for more than fifteen years, and even though life was hard, "filled with doubts about the wisdom of trying to wrestle a living from the land," soon the land and its spirit were in his blood. A bit like falling in love, his words reveal how deeply he came to care about the place and its people.

In 1894, when he caught a free train ride to Chicago to visit his sister, Siberts decided to stay for the winter, but he did not last, and soon enough concluded: "The Chicago people were a bad-mannered lot. They would shove and push each other around in a pretty bad way." So he headed home on the train.

"It was four o'clock in the morning when I pulled into Pierre. It felt good to be in South Dakota again. The air was good, and with all their faults, I liked the Dakota people." Siberts also discloses an acceptance and understanding of time and self in relation to the prairie.

"After a summer herding horses in South Dakota a man can get as much prairie and sky as he can stand. When that time comes, he has to go to town and blow off some steam, sit in the shade, and talk to some other human beings. I was in that shape in August 1899, and started out early to do something about it."

What did Bruce Siberts know that we have somehow forgotten? What sort of inner wisdom was he consulting as his guide? As Wayne Fanebust writes in *Tales of Dakota Territory*, within a chapter titled "Mystery of the Bones," "The land of the bright sun had a dark side. Like an unpredictable temptress, nature drew in the unsuspecting and unprepared. . . . Many of whom became her victims." Clearly, the prairie lands were not for the fainthearted, and to survive, individuals had to take careful note of the forces created by nature and circumstance that simply demanded their attention. Like Siberts, the settlers had to know when they simply could not take any more solitude—any more prairie and sky—and that required them to be in communication with their inner world as well as the world around them.

In other words, they had to work with Mother Nature, not against her, respecting her time line, her imposing presence in their lives, as nature did not allow its inhabitants to call the shots. According to Siberts, as reported by Wyman, "The weather of South Dakota at its worst is described as hotter than hell in the summer and colder than hell in the winter, and sometimes in the spring the wind blows like hell."

To peacefully coexist with nature, the pioneers had to develop a sixth sense: They had to display a willingness and an ability to conform to the wishes and demands of a power they could not match, understand, or conquer. And they had to somehow manage their personal needs in relation to the same unbeatable phenomenon.

In short, they had to build a bridge to themselves by considering their unique rhythms and impulses, but they also had to be in sync with the realities of prairie life. For sure, the pioneers had to learn how to bend with the demands of unseen forces, as prairie time, in a class of its own, did not fall in line with their requisitions or expectations.

Yet it is such a natural dimension that people of the prairie would not dream of keeping time any other way. Prairie time provides them with a cybernetic bridge to themselves, as people soon become one with the land, thinking and acting in rhythm to its magical beat.

Rosemary Radford Ruether, in *Meditations from the Wilderness* edited by Charles Brandt, states: "Return to the land means recovering something of the biorhythms of the body, the day, and the seasons from the world of clocks, computers, and artificial lighting that have almost entirely alienated us from these biorhythms."

You can see why man-made time lines are not an overly serious matter on the prairie. Since everyone senses the ultimate power of the "big clock," there is no mad scramble to get there first, and only the naive believe they can actually "beat the clock." But as you have probably concluded, that is good. People gladly succumb to the hypnotizing effect of the land, and in return, the open space, the rolling hills that act like an invisible force, shield and protect its inhabitants against the debilitating "hurry up and do it now" thinking of contemporary society.

The ultimate beauty of the prairie system, however, is that there is time—to dream and reflect, to listen and observe, to discover your own natural rhythm, to do less . . . to do more. Essentially speaking, there is time for matters of the heart. There is even time to doodle, a commonsense prescription for getting in touch with yourself. If you know how to draw and create genuine art, feel blessed, but for most of us, producing silly pictures and meaningless creations resembling absolutely nothing—plain old doodles—works just as well. The process is important, not the results.

Anything will do—pens, pencils, crayons, Magic Markers, whatever is handy—and feel free to write on what you can put your hands on: napkins, scratch paper, old newspapers, phone books, even the sole of your shoe, if that is all you can find.

The point is this: When you create art, even something very simple, your mind switches to neutral by focusing on something harmless and restful, and in that primitive act, you create a time cushion. Nothing more than tiny, thin slices of time, a time cushion is a place where you, and you alone, can pause briefly to get in touch with your internal clock. The prairie lands offer a similar remedy.

By providing a cushion—spacious, absorbent, comforting—the prairie shields its inhabitants from the harshness and excesses of modern-day society. Time seems irrelevant when you gaze out at the tall grasses waving back and forth with abandon, at a sky that is larger than life. As if time stopped long, long ago—no skyscrapers can be found, no bustling airports, and definitely no racing traffic or screaming police cars.

The prairie is an island unto itself, in a multitude of ways, and even though regular time-keeping mechanisms are everywhere, their impact is questionable, their efforts to control prairie residents nearly futile. For many prairie dwellers, time is something to be considered in the

Thoreauvian sense. As he wrote in *Walden:* "Time is but the stream I go a-fishing in. I drink at it; but while I drink I see the sandy bottom and detect how shallow it is. Its thin current slides away, but eternity remains. I would drink deeper; fish in the sky, whose bottom is pebbly with stars."

When time is scarce, when life's pressures get you down, try your hand at a doodle or two, especially when you cannot find any other way to put the charm, or the heart, back in your life, when you somehow managed to blow up that bridge to yourself instead of strengthening it. Do not let anyone laugh at you either: Prairie wisdom may look silly and strange, but since you know the story behind it, surely you will have the last laugh.

Wisdom is all around us
if we just take the time to discover it.

— MARK MCGINNIS,

"ELDERS OF THE FAITH,"

South Dakota Magazine

✍

CREATE RITUALS AND SAYINGS WITH HEART

Magical in nature, rituals thrive in prairie communities. Simple and unadorned but repeated over the years without fail, such acts build meaning and purpose into life in a way, and to a degree, that mystifies yet redeems. Without these absorbing, enjoyable, other-centered activities, life takes on a barren, colorless flavor. And there's something about repetition that prairie dwellers clearly appreciate.

One charming woman, tiny and brimming over with vitality—even while in her eighties—bakes more than fifty pies each summer with apples from her own tree just for the sheer pleasure of giving them away to friends and family. A man down the street freezes enough rhubarb to last a lifetime, then places an ad in the local paper to give the rest away. Yet another prairie resident stays up half the night making pickles and kuchen for his neighbors, the ones he likes anyway!

There is clearly something about the quiet prairie scene that encourages, gently but persistently, the pursuit of simple activities that, when repeated, become heartfelt, soul-enriching rituals. On the surface, such "habits" could appear to be less, even eccentric, yet wise prairie inhabitants understand the very human need to reach out, to share what they have with friends and family. To repeatedly do those things that have built-in meaning.

Many of them also understand the value of letting their hearts guide their decisions. In a world that produces a good deal of pragmatic, logical, cost-cutting deals, how refreshing to consider a place where people still value people, where the "process" doesn't take a backseat to the end result. Not automatically, anyway.

Consider, from a prairie perspective, the informal gathering of farmers and ranchers at the local coffee shop. Those arriving after six A.M. are met with remarks like: "Sleepin' in again, are ya?" . . . "Somebody sick in the family?" . . . "Truck givin' ya trouble?" . . . or "Wife got the flu?" Then a few well-meaning snickers followed by a contented sort of chatter marks the beginning of their day. Dead of winter, early spring, summer, late fall. It is always the same.

Early morning coffee—usually black as night—in a small cafe with whatever name you care to imagine. While I have never been to a cafe called The Main Stop, for some reason I can picture such a place, such a scene, on just about every surviving main street in small-town South Dakota. And no matter how many times this kind of scenario repeats itself, in no matter how many unpretentious-looking prairie cafes, a type of nonreligious "communion" occurs.

Without fanfare, certainly without undue planning or preparation, men, maybe a few women, of the prairie, in ritualistic fashion, join together in the early morning hours to gather and draw strength from their shared lifestyle, from their steady companionship, to share stories of home and family, to renew bonds of faith, loyalty, and love. While almost always unspoken, caring radiates from their camaraderie; genuine concern springs from their regular get-togethers, making each day a tiny bit brighter, each individual's journey a bit easier, a bit more pleasant.

What about the early morning walk, the evening stroll to the local ice cream shop, or collecting and storing sacks of walnuts in the fall? Simple pastimes, when repeated often enough, take on special meaning and purpose. By reminding us of our need for stability, predictability, and soul-wise pursuits, these routine activities comfort our frazzled nerves, repair our often frayed, twenty-first-century heartstrings, and help sustain our connection to each other, ourselves, and the world.

A PRAIRIE PICNIC

I remember well a family picnic to celebrate spring. Nothing elaborate, nothing contrived, just "C'mon, we have got to celebrate the arrival of a new season after a long, gray winter." Held on the banks of the Missouri River, winter's snow, dusty and frozen and still visible by the shoreline, this sort of unpretentious gathering was filled with heart, the nurturing effect on our sagging winter spirits truly spectacular. But being people of the prairie, our expectations were reasonable, something that helps any event succeed—especially the simple ones. Perhaps that is yet another important dimension of the prairie lifestyle: Rituals with the ability to sustain our hearts and souls are best enjoyed and appreciated when kept simple and low-key. By asking so little of us, the return is most always considerable.

For one thing, prairie rituals often involve nature and the vast outdoors; sometimes they involve the inspiring rituals of other living creatures. One soul-wise woman rises early in the morning, especially in the spring, just to watch and listen to the birds. Like Thoreau, is it possible that she, like many other prairie dwellers, believes in a perfect correspondence between the inner nature of man and the structure of the external world, between the soul and nature?

Nature, to Thoreau being the materialization of spirit and a physical realization of divinity, referred to it as a sacred place worthy of man's respect and awe. As he wrote in his chapter called "Solitude" in *Walden*: "There can be no very black melancholy to him who lives in the midst of Nature and has his senses still."

Not surprisingly, the prairie itself can seem like nature's belly, if there is such a thing. The unassuming lands, poetic and sometimes wishful in bearing, gently encourage us to notice all of nature: its rich display of color, its contentment, its triumphs and its sorrows. Too often discounted as trivial or trite, the absolute genius of nature is all too evident in the middle of nowhere. Since there is less competition for limited and overburdened attention spans, people of the prairie take note of events, ceremonies, even parades, that nature, and nature alone, provides. And in their watching, rituals of magical, if not mystical proportions come into focus; they are born, sustained, and, quite literally, handled with tremendous care.

HEARTFELT SAYINGS

The power of words, noted for centuries by scholars all around the globe, is no less important or compelling on the rolling prairie. The people, the culture, and the place are set off by a vernacular that silhouettes the country lifestyle while accenting the rather intrepid nature of the genuine South Dakota native with amazing clarity and charm. A few fad-type words manage to penetrate the prairie screening process, but overall, "talk" is down to earth, the no-frills approach.

Fast talkers, smooth talkers, or, heaven forbid, talkers with a pretentious air are surely suspect, and as they are quickly scrutinized by the longtime prairie resident, it becomes apparent that prairie folk are nobody's fool. They value honest communication and a straightforward manner; a friendly demeanor, genuine and true, helps, too.

Within this context is a built-in appreciation for words that inspire: heartfelt sayings passed down through the generations like rare gems worthy of our continued belief and preservation. Providing a path for the young, the newcomer, or the lost and confused, prairie sayings, some old, some new, add depth and pizzazz to an otherwise quiet scene.

THE EARLY DAYS

My grandmother's favorite expressions, "Keep the peace" and "Keep a song in your heart," come to mind. A truly authentic prairie woman born Christmas Eve of 1889 in Cuthbert, South Dakota, she was also fond of saying, "It will all come out in the wash." A rather short, stout lady with little regard for fashion or foolishness, Anna outlived all but one of her seven brothers and sisters, coming to her final rest just two days shy of ninety-eight; and now, her advice and encouragement linger on, finding purpose, earthly renewal, in the pages of this book. Born on her birthday, in 1954, I loved her very much, knew her well, and so, I think she would approve. Always supportive and genuine, she also would have applauded my efforts as an author; I her granddaughter, who shared her sweet tooth, loved to discuss the "ways of the world" with anyone who would listen, even at an early age.

Much like the rolling hills of the prairie, Anna's ways—her sayings, her lifestyle, her commitment to family and humankind—are truly timeless in their capacity to inspire others. And even though she spoke of the prairie fire that destroyed their newly built frame house when she was in her teens and her father's unexpected death before his fortieth birthday, her outlook was still sunny in a peaceful sort of way.

I could see it in the way she lived, feel it in the way she looked at me, hear it in her words. To me, her daily routine, peaceful gaze, and gentle speech reflected a softness born of strength; she delighted in the joy of others, seemed to possess a deep contentment, to be at peace with herself and the universe. I think some people envied that quality in her, when, to me, even as a young girl, I felt drawn to it; it gave me silent reassurance that everything would work out okay. That no matter what, she would be there. Her love was constant, like a ray of sunlight in my life, and she seemed to feel no malice of heart toward anyone. I admired that most about her.

With no illusions about hard times, she had endured plenty, but Anna remained true to her prairie spirit until the end.

She loved life for what it could reasonably offer, finding refuge in nature: Her garden brimmed over with hollyhocks, pink, white, red, and purple; her tall, stately, walnut tree; her bountiful blackberry tree; her apple trees; the changing seasons; the everyday habits of robins and squirrels. Anna also found comfort in her music as she played the piano and fiddle by ear. Seated at her old upright, her wrinkled hands performing without fail, she would begin with a rousing rendition of "Turkey in the Straw," moving into "When Irish Eyes Are Smiling" or "You Are My Sunshine." I loved to sit beside her when she played, as I was a young piano student at the time. She often listened to me practice. And I can see her now as she waltzed through a thick volume of Alfred Tennyson's poetry—another of her small treasures that I found so fascinating.

From this bountiful existence came a happy heart. Made famous by the children in her neighborhood—she loved to share the apples from her fruit trees or build a small bonfire in her yard for their marshmallows—Anna cherished the underling. Always glad to send a few dollars to a favorite charity, she took pleasure in using her resources wisely so others might benefit. Through her kindness, she inspired others to keep going despite setbacks or loss; through her words and deeds, her wonderful prairie heart lives on.

Not given to self-pity or self-indulgence, from her I learned the value of making the best out of any situation: As the old saying goes, if you have lemons, make lemonade.

Yet she is not the only one to understand the importance of living well—to be at peace with nature, your surroundings, and those around you; to share wisdom, caring, and love; to make simple acts of kindness a priority. And, in Anna's case, to allow others into your heart unconditionally. Nearly everyone can repeat a few "wise" words from memory; unique or not, heartfelt sayings passed down through the generations keep us in touch with ideas that never grow stale. They bring us down to earth when our common sense has disappeared like a strong March wind, when we overintellectualize a problem or deny our feelings and thereby forget our hearts and souls in the process.

The prairie culture, in particular, takes special care to keep such sayings alive and circulating; new sayings are born each day. Some manage to survive the test of time.

In talking with longtime residents about their favorite phrases, many of which you will recognize, I recorded a few to share and hopefully remember:

> *Friends are good but family is what counts.*
> *She has nothing to do and all day to do it in.*
> *Into every life a little rain must fall.*
> *A place for everything, and everything in its place.*

Waste not, want not.

Watch the pennies, the dollars will take care of themselves.

Early to bed, early to rise, will make you healthy, wealthy, and wise.

The early bird gets the worm.

Always carry on, the best you can.

Leave it to Mother Nature.

Worry less, do more.

Keep the spirit.

Good fortune is a matter of perspective.

And from A.B. "Bud" Tyler, Jr., (1910–1999) internationally known polo player and family friend: "The nicest thing you can give anyone is a smile, and it doesn't cost a dime."

We must march my darlings, we must bear the brunt of danger,

We the youthful sinewy races, all the rest on us depend,

Pioneers! O pioneers!

—WALT WHITMAN,

"PIONEERS! O PIONEERS!"

TRY ALMOST ANYTHING ONCE

In a flourishing contemporary society, options and choices, things to do and see, are endless. This is especially true of urban areas, where no matter how narrow a particular interest, there is nearly always someone else to link up with. From finding a group dedicated to yoga or the martial arts to locating those who like to ski-dive, scuba-dive, or drive a race car, check the yellow pages or just ask around. It is that simple.

Remote corners of the world, isolated villages, teeny-tiny towns, and, of course, prairie-based communities, including those who reside on the prairie itself miles and miles from another living soul, experience a different reality: a narrow menu, a short availability list, an "outside the mainstream" set of options. In such contexts it is doubtful you will find a formal class on archery, mountain climbing, how to play the harp or the bagpipes, the history of ragtime, Buddhism, or anything else your imagination conjures up that is on the unique side.

You might, however, find an informal group dedicated to square dancing; you might find a fishing class or a horseback riding club. Maybe there are a few people who like to hunt for arrowheads, a group of historians interested in revitalizing local traditions of old. With any luck you can find a few people dedicated to books, storytelling, rodeo, hunting, boats, gardening, playing cards, cake decorating, knitting or sewing, walking, swimming, or aerobics. Maybe. But some places on the prairie are so completely remote (desolate, in the eyes of some) that you will not find any of the above. Farms, ranches, and homes can be a good thirty to sixty to ninety miles away from anything besides a lonely tree at the end of a dusty gravel road. The isolation can be crushing, truly devastating if you pine for the companionship of anyone besides a family member, a cherished pet, or nature.

In O. E. Rölvaag's *Giants in the Earth: A Saga of the Prairie*, a classic that begins, "To those of my people who took part in the great settling, to them and their generations I dedicate this narrative," the loneliness of the prairie comes through in riveting detail: "In the dead of winter, of course, when the blizzards are raging and we don't see any folks for weeks at a time, she has days when she seems to go all to pieces; but I hardly reckon that as the disease—that sort of thing happens to a good many of us, let me tell you!"

A more recent description of prairie life paints this picture: "When you are born on the edge of the plains, you spend your life clinging to it, praying that you won't fall off."

Appearing as an essay in *Leaning into the Wind*, a work edited by Linda Hasselstrom, Gaydell Collier, and Nancy Curtis, contributor Robyn Carmichael Eden goes on to write: "But we are stubborn optimists, never thinking we won't survive. The land is our trial, our comfort, and ultimately, our identity." Within the same book, Katherine Wood writes in a poem called "Plains Preponderance": "Then the dry spring wind comes up billowing dust across the farm-perfect view, swirling dirt against the Jeep, making her feel desolate, almost crazy for no reason." Wood continues, coming to refer to the dust as a "layered curtain of prairie gold" while conveying a strong sense of continuity: Has the prairie experience really changed over the years?

Sod huts no longer dot the landscape; herds of buffalo no longer roam freely across the great prairie expanse; the Native American culture has undergone a tremendous amount of change; the horse-and-buggy era is only a memory. Yet the prairie's essence, its soul and curious force, lies untouched. It still features a sparse population; a people, who, as a whole, are of a kind and friendly nature; a vast land that is primarily unfenced, generally uninhabited. Nature, weather, livestock and grain prices, rough-and-tumble politics, hunting and fishing are still the name of the game.

Driving along an isolated highway, looking out at an endless stretch of prairie, noticing the way the sky dominates the entire scene and maybe catching a glimpse of a renegade pheasant darting around like a nervous diplomat still brings tears to my eyes even though I grew up with the prairie at my side. Never tiring of its comfort, only feeling confused and frustrated at times by its constant pull on my heart and soul, to me the prairie, the lifestyle built around its mystical and mesmerizing presence, the entire package—people, place, history, and culture—remains, even today, curiously poetic.

In the sense that there is a beautiful rhythm to the unchanging yet dynamic landscape, to the prairie's knowing spirit, to its uninhibited nature; in the sense that I do love this place: this place where my heart resides.

Change is a relative commodity on the prairie, and generally speaking, time marches on with little to no effect on the place itself: You are right to conclude that scarcity is still the general rule. So you will not find (excluding the handful of communities that are, technically, cities) an extensive list of functions, activities, clubs, or entertainment outlets neatly formed, prepackaged, and arranged just so.

Therein, of course, lies the nugget of wisdom that is the focus of this chapter: Try almost anything once.

A SLIGHTLY DIFFERENT MENU

One of the most intriguing aspects of prairie life comes to light within this framework, this idea of trying the unplanned, the unexpected, or the undesired at least once. Primarily because of the outward limitations imposed on the area due to geography and otherwise, life on the prairie seems to demand it. Those who live there understand and value the need to be creative and resourceful when it comes to spending time with friends, sharing resources, developing interests and hobbies, finding "interesting" things to do.

Some, primarily those who have not experienced the area firsthand for any length of time, prematurely conclude that the prairie lands are stark and barren, therefore lacking in opportunity. Yet it is just a matter of being open to a slightly different menu, a new style or an unusual twist. There may be fewer options and choices, in total, but that, too, is the beauty of the prairie experience.

By being open to trying *most* things at least once, self-discovery lies right around the nearest corner. As many of the pioneers believed, an adventuresome spirit can spell the difference between stagnation, a life devoid of heart and joy, and true happiness. And even though their motivations were varied, sometimes complex, most of them seemed to sense the ultimate value in moving beyond the safety net of a world that was already settled, orderly, and predictable. The lure of the great unknown, a powerful force indeed, led them inward, geographically and spiritually. And so it is today, as a pioneer of the twenty-first century, that you can travel inward to console the part of yourself that feels lost and unsure, nearly numb from the excess of modern-day society, practically frozen by fear, frustration, and strife; you can look in new directions, burgeoning with energy, for answers—for hope.

Prairie life, the place and its people, continues to offer important, life-enhancing clues by embracing, requiring, and supporting a lifestyle that remains outside the mainstream in so many ways; instead of running from its foreign qualities, its subtle shape and unique contour, because you imagine the prairie's time has already come and gone (who wants to go backward!), you have much to gain by submerging yourself in the prairie's mysterious currents. By opening your heart to the ways of old, the ways of the prairie and its people, you may come to realize the inherent limitations of that which is novel, flamboyant, or exciting, especially in the prepackaged sense.

PRAIRIE PASTIMES

Doing "strange" things, charting a different course every now and then, is critical for a happy heart, a strong mind, a vital spirit. This is true regardless of age, gender, lifestyle, or income. But when the options are excessive, when the choices are never ending, there is a tendency to drown in our own abundance. It makes sense after all.

Much like children skipping through a bright, tantalizing, candy store, saying no becomes increasingly difficult, and while those who suffer from having too much don't know which way to turn, those who suffer from having too little feel ashamed and dejected, like aliens on a planet they no longer understand or appreciate.

By offering simple fare, a back-to-the-basics approach, the prairie lifestyle manages to reduce the massive gap between too much and too little, allowing the "inevitable classlessness of prairie life" (Heat-Moon, *PrairyErth*) to exert itself. And within this "flattened" terrain and perspective, prairie natives have learned to open themselves to a way of thinking and behaving that keeps them growing and young despite the perceived limitations of the area.

They have learned to "try almost anything once."

NEWCOMERS

Those who move to the area from drastically different environments, even some who are returning "home," may come to this understanding slowly as opposed to quickly. A few truly panic at the sight of such a "thrown wide open" landscape; others suffer from months or years of "culture shock" as they frantically try to re-create what was customary for them in another place, another land, another time. As Robyn Eden points out in *Leaning into the Wind*:

In the vast prairie hyperspace, there is no room for clutter. Those who call the prairie boring and empty are those who pass through quickly, moving from one densely inhabited place to another, senses so dulled they need the neon gratification of mountains or seas or deserts. Born into a world of sensory overload, they are blind to the low-light vision of the plains. Used to perpetual motion, they cannot stand still long enough to feel the pull of roots just below the surface of the undulating grasslands.

But as she also points out: "The human offspring of the prairie are different at birth. Others spend lifetimes desperately seeking what we are born knowing."

How true it is that newcomers are often overwhelmed by the "basics," confounded by the lack of "apparent" options, and, quite frankly, annoyed by the simplicity.

One woman, when she moved to the area from a city, put it this way: "I felt like someone had dropped me right off the face of the earth." Referring to her new residency in a remote part of South Dakota, you can be sure she speaks for others as well. But eventually a transformation occurs: The disgruntled (or perplexed) newcomer, after sinking into the prairie lifestyle for a time, discovers merit in the perceived strangeness, in their personal encounter with the annoying emptiness. And with all that that implies, this sort of *change* can be magnificent, truly eye-opening.

What is the catalyst, you ask, or is it simply a matter of holding still for a time while the prairie works its magic on your heart and soul?

In my humble estimation, conversion of this magnitude stems from a convergence of forces not easily isolated or understood. But for starters consider the eventual realization: The prairie, the people and the lifestyle, must be appreciated for what it offers, not disliked so much for its perceived shortcomings. This kind of acceptance can take time, especially for those who are resolutely opposed to making the transition. But once this development takes hold, the "city person" cautiously ventures out to the Fourth of July day rodeo; or maybe he picks up a fishing pole for the first time ever; quite possibly, she decides to learn how to play whist (a popular card game in South Dakota). Or maybe someone offers to teach her how to make chokecherry jelly, how to dance to a country tune, how to ride a spirited horse in the next parade down Main Street. Everyday pastimes are made brand new: a joyful process in every sense of the word. For the newcomer, you can almost see the relief, the happiness; you can certainly feel it.

While it *may* be less than an actual "rebirth," this process of learning to let go and try almost anything once is more special than you might suspect. Because in the process of trying new things, activities you may never have wanted to try in the first place, surprising abilities and dormant interests readily develop into something more.

At first, this kind of transformation may overwhelm you in the most positive sense: Like a surprise you never expected (not in the slightest!), your heart may race, your smile will likely say it all. And if you are truly wise, you will come to thank the prairie lands for forcing you to reach inside for a new reality, for bringing your spirit to life once again in ways no one could or would have predicted. For giving you a reason to smile.

Watching children at play in the snow, their happy squeals capture your attention and your heart. You smile or wave; you nod in appreciation for their happy state of mind. Maybe you reach down to make a snowball of your very own, then toss it toward a nearby tree just to watch it splatter and fall to the ground. Quite simply, it's fun. And trying new things, especially simple, life-preserving activities served up on the prairie, can also be fun. Not surprisingly, as a new interest catches hold, as you nurture it along, it may gracefully evolve into an absorbing passion that stimulates growth, happiness, and inner peace—another form of personal wealth.

The prairie lands offer all this and more. In the guise of "nothing-ness," they gently but persistently force us to consider simple activities and pastimes anew. Because, as you now understand, *that's all there is*. But as you relinquish a bit of your stubbornness, surrender to that which appears strange or curiously lacking, you may come to understand your-self better. You may feel rejuvenated and joyful as you once again realize that less is more, a powerful, prairie-wise belief.

Most important, as you let a bit of the prairie's wisdom seep into your heart, you may see the road map a bit more clearly: *this road map to the heart.*

The silence of the Plains,
this great unpeopled landscape of earth and sky,
is much like the silence one finds in a monastery,
an unfathomable silence that has the power to re-form you.

— KATHLEEN NORRIS,
Dakota

CULTIVATE A
QUIET SENSE OF PURPOSE

Have you ever tried to imagine a world without so much noise, a world without chaos, confusion, or corruption? Where might it be, what might it look like, why might it exist? And most important, what might you do there?

These sorts of private musings, common to most, reveal our innate need for calm; they underlie our ongoing search for what is real. In many ways, a desire for greater harmony and peace in our everyday lives is reminiscent of daydreams, of graceful, delicately swift butterflies flitting around in a dreamy display of color. In contrast, our movements and actions, in capturing our human limitations so grandly, appear uncoordinated and slightly inglorious. We limp; we sag; we sometimes drag about like poorly performing puppets. Thus it is natural to yearn for a smoother existence, to imagine a more tranquil setting in which to play out the days of our lives.

People of the remote prairie lands—past and present—experience a reality somewhat more along these lines. And while it is not a carefree existence in any sense of the word, a certain amount of serenity is bound to emanate from a place that features native grasses brightly accented by a heavenly light—reams of golden rays, or by night, a blanket of brilliant stars—wildlife, wildflowers, and stretches of clear, clean water. Does it sound inviting, peaceful, and otherworldly?

But to those who settled the land, a first encounter with the prairie often caused them to venture "timidly into the edges of the grass," clinging to the "outriders of forest like mice hugging a wall. For this was alien land, not only in physical appearance but in its harsh rejection of familiar custom; it diminished men's works and revealed them to a vast and critical sky, and forced people into new ways of looking at the land and themselves, and changed them forever."

John Madson, in *Where the Sky Began: Land of the Tallgrass Prairie*, goes on to write: "The world had opened into a light-filled wilderness of sky and grass that would open its people as well, freeing them of certain dogma, breaking old institutions, and shaping new ones to fit the land."

That was then. Now, however, as we come full circle in our quest for new territories to explore, this "alien land" reaches out to us like an old and deeply trusted friend, quietly calming our fears, gently whispering our names; a beacon of light stretched out before us, a place that has weathered the storm.

This transformation—how truly incredible. What was once a source of fear has come to mean much more; in fact, we find ourselves cherishing what is left of the great prairie lands, clinging to them as if their death may somehow precede ours. Like a final visage of the past, symbolic of our desire to stretch as a nation, to advance, when the prairie is gone, something deep within us may cry out with a shrillness of heart: *Don't leave us behind; we need you.*

THE INSIDE STORY

How have these lands come to mean so much—to me and to those who notice, those who care? Indeed, how has the prairie wormed its way into our hearts, with us barely noticing at all? And how has this transformed us in the process?

Wayne Fanebust, in *Tales of Dakota Territory*, described the prairie as a "place nature created to test the brave and crush the weak and foolhardy." So how did so many come to love this place with all its bumps and blemishes? Indescribable beauty played a role, as did a sense of total freedom. O. E. Rölvaag, in *Giants in the Earth*, captures the breathtaking beauty quite eloquently.

But it may happen that toward evening, just as the day is nearly done, a curtain is suddenly drawn aside; in the western sky appears a window— not built by the hand of man—all luminous with splendour; out of it shines a radiance clearer and more glorious than anything the eye has ever beheld; all around the window night and darkness hang suspended like draperies—they too radiating a glory not of this world.

Obviously, the prairie offers its own brand of rewards: It encourages those who live there to come to terms with who they are and what they believe. You can't hide from the prairie; you can't hide from yourself. And eventually, if you stay there long enough, you join hands with the land—its glorious side, its dark side, its side you don't quite understand. This union, the dynamic it creates, has a particular effect on residents, causing some to appear "dry," even a bit crusty; it is as if the intense seasons, tough times, and dusty roads have taken their toll. Prairie people, a unique lot to be sure, can be most unnerving, especially for the "outsider" who is not accustomed to their ways.

Baffled by their calm exteriors that seem to be matched by equally serene interiors, by smiles that are sometimes slow to surface, by their casual attention to material effects, some decide, albeit prematurely, that prairie residents are slightly jaded or provincial. Not really. They have just learned a few things along the way.

One woman who lived in the central part of South Dakota for sixty-four years said she grew to appreciate the plains with their ever changing light and its effect upon the landscape. A senior citizen, now 101, explained how life on the prairie taught her about the value of "long-range views." And Frances Nickel Jones, 104 years of age, points out how the prairie taught her "patience." In 1920, one gentleman, in writing a letter (as excerpted in *Where the Sky Began* by John Madson) described the considerable effect of the plains this way: "It had taken the shrillness out of them. They had learned the trick of quiet."

Even today, even now, the prairie has a similar effect on people: It brings them closer to themselves. Like a gentle backdrop to our "busyness," the prairie provides a sense of stability, natural beauty, and peace. It truly helps us learn the trick of quiet, as aptly put a good eighty years ago. And from this kind of perspective there is much to be gained. I am, in fact, reminded of the ants and bees, furiously at work to ensure their basic survival.

When we finally grow quiet, when we pause at least briefly to reflect and ponder life, its wonders and mysteries, its force and power, its magical way of taking us exactly where we need to be when we least expect it, we begin to understand how we are a reflection of those ants and bees; and in our mirrorlike dimension it becomes even more apparent how stately and grand the prairie lands are in comparison. Within this image, this sharp contrast between deep, abiding calm and perpetual zaniness (as our actions can appear), there is something to be gleaned beyond the obvious.

A QUIET SENSE OF PURPOSE

Look inside your soul; look inside your heart. Did you find a sense of peace or one of panic? Feelings of confusion, chaos, or calm? Joy or pain? While the answers may be strangely elusive, they are usually there if you listen, if you truly want to hear them. But when was the last time you stood still long enough to even probe the true depths of your heart and soul? And did you like what you found?

Those who reside on the prairie for any length of time, by conjuring up internal visions of that which surrounds them in their everyday life, seem to be magically in tune with their inner resources: their heart and soul, the truest of true, the internal barometers we insist on ignoring in exchange for external indicators lacking precision, courage, and wisdom.

Like the cowardly lion in the *Wonderful Wizard of Oz*, we are taken in by razzle-dazzle fads; we are scared to death of things that go bump in the night; we shiver at the sight of our very own shadow. *We look to others to lead the way.* And all because we are unduly captivated by the wrong indicators, because we substitute society's props for what lies within us—free of charge, authentic, multidimensional, and literally overflowing with meaning and purpose. Prairie dwellers, however, often find themselves in the midst of a different reality.

"Things" are simply not as abundant on the grasslands, nor do they take center stage when available. There is a natural cautiousness on the prairie, a desire to honor what is real, what is tested and true. As a carryover from the days of the pioneers, people seem to trust hardship more than materialistic distractions of any brand or variety. And most respect and trust the strength of their prairie surroundings and heritage to the point where man-made objects, no matter how magnificent, no matter how impressive, have a difficult time competing for their attention and affection.

When there is love in your heart—love of the land, love of nature, love of family and friends—external objects, while they can be a source of great inspiration and pleasure, do not take on undue meaning; they do not become a cheap and senseless substitute for what is real. Thus, on the prairie lands I grew up with, there is a quiet sense of purpose among the people. It comforts them, acting as an invisible buffer, a silent protector, against the onslaught of media and hype dished out by a sophisticated, twenty-first-century world.

From this "quiet sense of purpose" perspective springs an intuitive understanding of the need to shun pretentious ways that alienate and divide, sealing people off from one another, from themselves, as well, by cutting them off from their innermost needs, from what their hearts are frantically trying to tell them.

This lack of pretense is often misunderstood by the outsider, however. Mistaken for dullness or a lack of distinction, sometimes perceived as naiveté or taken to suggest a lack of intelligence or education, prairie people are subjected to a variety of derogatory and generally incorrect assumptions about who and what they are. Yet most take it all in stride, realizing that surface impressions do not reveal the truth of any matter. They also realize that pleasing themselves, indeed, *being themselves*, provides them with a quiet sort of confidence, a knowing outlook on life, a centered and balanced perspective upon which to build a life or a dream. Much like the well-built foundation of an exquisite physical structure, these people, especially those who have resided there for some time, are rock solid where it counts, so jeers—silent, spoken, deserved, or undeserved—from outsiders hold very little power over them.

Comfortable with a lifestyle that literally "grew up on the prairie," these people adorn themselves in basic fashions (most out-of-date regardless of income); they drive old cars or pickups for the most part; they live in modest homes; they prepare basic, healthy food; they go to movies on a seldom, don't-have-to-see-it-right-now basis; they take plenty of walks in the evening, stopping to chat with neighbors and friends; they bend over backward to help those in need; they talk to each other on a regular basis; they enjoy nature, outdoor activities, as frequently as possible.

They keep it simple: sometimes because they have to, sometimes because they want to, but always because they value what they have, even if the outside world, trapped in elements of make-believe, doesn't quite understand. Outsiders, sometimes caught up in all the gift wrap, don't realize that prairie dwellers insist on opening the package to discover the true contents: of life, the substance of the matter, if you will. A natural habit for most, these people are not easily fooled by the artificial, the expensive, or the ornate.

As such, I can't help but believe that we, regardless of gender, race, religion, income, career interests, or age, have something to learn from these people. They are not dull.

SPACE, FREEDOM, AND CONTENTMENT:
A QUIET SENSE OF PURPOSE

Mark Peterson, a Lutheran pastor living in Buffalo, South Dakota, wrote about the "Wide Open Space" for *South Dakota Magazine*. His words convey an appreciation for what is there, even though it may appear to be "less" by those who do not understand life with the land.

Occasionally the mid-morning sun is obscured by a racing cloud and my squinting eyes can open to take in more fully the expanse that surrounds me. I can see to the horizon maybe 50 miles away. Brown grass is bent over and bobbing like a rushing river on both sides of me. . . . Such wide open space surrounds me and the wind, the breath of the prairie herself, grabs at me and pushes my car. . . . It is overbearing. As a city boy, transplanted here not more than a few years ago, I found it a difficult transition. So much sky, so vast a prairie, such force of wind. There is no escape. . . . This prairie knows me; there is no way to escape her relentless gaze. . . . Living under her daily gaze has left me with no alternative. There is communion. I have come to find that there is an unspoken bond between this wind, this landscape, and those who live here constantly surrounded in her relentless grasp. A trinity, one might say. Though I try without success to maintain some sort of distance, it is a futile effort. . . . These wide open spaces rip open my soul. She can see deep within. She knows who I am and where I am going, perhaps better than myself. This can be intimidating—being known in such a way. . . . As I look back, I now know that my several months of anxiety upon arrival to this area was a result of this prairie herself. Her deep blue eyes, her brown etched skin sinking deeply into my being. . . . Though I still try to hide, it comes as a difficult realization that I will endlessly be known by her.

Legend has it that Jesse James jumped across a wide and deadly chasm

in the rocks near Garretson, South Dakota, while evading pursuers.

The chasm is called Devil's Gulch. . . . Devil's Gulch is one of those

unlikely features on the prairie. It shows up with great suddenness.

— W A Y N E   F A N E B U S T ,

Tales of Dakota Territory,

V O L U M E   I

～

STRIKE OUT
ON YOUR OWN

Freedom: an American statement, an envied condition by many, a word that rings with emotion and choice, an elusive goal, a fantasy perhaps. As a whole, we are a people who admire staying power and commitment just as much as we relish the idea of being free to follow our heart's desire; thus, we are forced to play a tough balancing act between our dependent and our independent sides. And often enough, we are unsuccessful in our attempt to find peace and harmony within this challenging, ever-changing context.

I am reminded of the married couple desperately trying to accommodate each other's need for freedom, at least in some measure, while at the same moment wanting to hold each other close. Love can be a confusing, sometimes overpowering emotion, causing us to wonder and worry about its very expression, its motives and purposes.

The prairie lands are in many ways a reflection of this dichotomy: They confine while simultaneously offering a sense of unabridged freedom. As one longtime resident put it, there is something about prairie life that fosters a sense of independence; there is always a desire to see what is over the next hill. Yet these same prairie lands, once in your heart and soul, hold you quietly in place, making their place known and felt forever.

Listen to these prairie-wise voices as selected from essays appearing in *Leaning into the Wind, Women Write from the Heart of the West*:

From my childhood on the frontier I got the soul of an adventurer, and I spent the rest of my life finding ways to move into new directions.
—PHYLLIS LUMAN METAL, "I CARRY THE RANCH INSIDE ME"

Our values and spirit are formed by the place we live.
—BONNIE LARSON STAIGER

Her poem, "A Sense of Place," goes like this:

Given the choice
I would walk
every measured mile
of the contoured prairie
take up a handful of earth
knowing it's time to plant
by the smell of the soil
kick gravel stones
along the section line
and startle a meadowlark
off her grass-covered nest
count redwings in the cattails
unearth a Lakota fire ring
and give thanks to the four winds

And you have to understand that I love this place. It is my home. I am free and bound. If that sounds a dichotomy, you have not caught the proper balance; I could not be secure if I were not allowed freedom. I have to have room to think and to call upon the strength I take from solitude. I have to run to the hills and look into the sweep of prairie and the river and the distance and I have to leave here and I have to come back.

— JOAN HOFFMAN, "HOME ON THE RANGE"

We still stand under the stars and talk about faith and loss and dreams, and we are still teenage Western girls who grew up free.

— KAREN OBRIGEWITCH, "GROWING UP FREE"

The prairie is in me like the dirt is in the earth—or in the mulberries.

— BERNIE KOLLER, "MULBERRIES"

I love the land so much I feel joined to it. As you walk over the prairies and hills, walk softly, for you tread on my soul. . . . This is my history and future, the wind blows so fierce it might blow through my veins.

— PATTY LITZEL, "GIFTS FROM THE SKY"

Do you hear the deep emotions running through these words? Do you feel the love expressed for a place too often discounted as empty and barren? The fierce independence running through the souls of these women despite and because of their deep connection to the land?

Put your ear to the ground. . . . *Listen.*

STAKE A CLAIM

During the spring and summer months wild prairie flowers are eager to stake a claim on the land. Almost like a sudden gift of fate, they appear in random order, scattered here and there as if someone with fairy dust in her heart dropped a basket of seed for the wind to scatter with total abandon. All colors, shapes, and sizes, from the petite-looking pasque-flower (the state flower, also called prairie smoke) in the spring to yellow star grass and daisies of all varieties in the summer, the prairie scene radiates a noticeable vibrancy as the weather warms.

As if anxious to make their mark, prairie flowers surprise many visitors with their determined presence amid the thick, free-flowing prairie grasses. Even during the intense heat of summer, with the long dry spells and backbreaking wind that blows like it will never, never stop, the native flowers march on. Part of the prairie's mystique, indeed, the tiny, timid flowers of spring (the pasqueflower often emerges before the last snow can clear the land) gradually give way to tall, sturdy-looking varieties in yellow, gold, and purple that blend with the native grasses as if an artist's brush had just graced a massive outdoor set with incredible imagination. With indescribable passion.

The wildflowers of the prairie add to the feeling of freedom that floats through the air like the fluffy white cotton of the cottonwood tree. Truly intoxicating, more than nearly anything man-made, there is nothing contrived or pretentious about a bright show of color blending in, almost unnoticeably at times, with a scene straight out of *Little House on the Prairie* by Laura Ingalls Wilder.

Yet at the very same precise moment, the native prairie flowers seem to say, "I am here to stay. This is where I belong. This land is part of me. I will *never* leave."

As if they have effectively staked their claim, just like the pioneers and settlers of old, these colorful gems—snow white and sunshine yellow—know their place; they know the value of staying close to the land.

Where the Heart Resides

Like the people who inhabit the area, these flowers, tiny or showy or somewhere in between, offer us insight and inspiration. Being a survivor has its rewards and pluses. Being a pleasant contrast to the not-so-pleasant side of life can be joyful and exhilarating. Being beautiful and uplifting and lovely is worthwhile. Being low in maintenance can be truly perfect. Being natural and carefree—well, what could be better?

FOLLOW YOUR HEART

What, I wonder, was in the heart of hearts of a settler back in the mid to late 1800s? Sure, we have all read our history books—we know what we think we know—but do we really know the heart and soul of the average pioneer? Reluctant or enthused? Frozen with fear or moving forward with hope, courage, and commitment?

There are those who believe the great majority of settlers headed west out of economic necessity; that they hated the uncertainty, danger, and daily strife of trying to survive on the unsettled, barren-looking prairie lands offering the seldom tree, a rare rain shower, a desert-type sun, a merciless wind, and in the winter, blinding snow sent down from above to freeze and punish all living creatures. A place created to intimidate the few brave souls daring to venture forth into the prairie's daunting sphere. Yet something tells me there had to be more.

People who choose to climb Mount Everest, who set their sights on professional baseball, who take on any steep challenge have something in common: a passion for the task ahead, a deep love for whatever has captured their heart, a burning desire to push themselves beyond normal endurance levels—to test their strength and ability and commitment. It seems to me that a good number of the settlers must have felt like this, otherwise, how could they have prevailed when the deck was obviously stacked in favor of the prairie?

It seems incomprehensible to me to write off their often heroic efforts as an economic necessity. Worse yet, it feels like a disservice of incredible magnitude to downplay their accomplishment—amazing, admirable, and absolute—for any reason.

Regardless of why, irrespective of the variety of motivations that came into play, we need to remember and honor their journey into the unknown. By discounting what they endured to make new lives for themselves, we only grow more cynical and disenchanted. Viewed in a more realistic light, it is safe to say that the pioneer spirit, a desire to strike out on one's own despite the odds and inevitable hardship, is worth emulating; it is surely worth rekindling such genuine desire in our hearts. And even though this may be difficult to do in a geographical sense, emotionally, spiritually, and intellectually it is not; the issues of today are just as challenging, if not more so.

To do otherwise, however, is to shrink from life out of fear, to become less with each passing generation. Who will our children be inspired by, if not by us? What will our country become if we stop reaching for the stars, stop pushing ourselves to dig deeper for the very meaning of life—the rich core from which wondrous truths derive?

What are we waiting for, I wonder. And why are we so captivated, so entirely taken in by violence—on every screen, in every book, in homes, schools, and playgrounds. To me, it is a mystery of immense proportions: When life *can* be grand and beautiful, we choose to make it less; we denigrate our very existence with senseless, hateful acts reflecting our true discontent like the most accurate thermometer in the universe. Like robots without hearts, souls, or minds, we seem unable to stop, incapable of changing our direction, even while the rewards are quite invisible, the damage all too visible. And no matter what parents do as caring, deeply concerned individuals, society and peer groups are the paramount influences to be reckoned with.

KINDRED SPIRITS

Again, we look to the prairie—the place and its people—for hints and, yes, for wisdom. When asked "What makes South Dakota special?" one person replied: "The people, the majority of South Dakotans have an innate kindness." Perhaps it is because the people are not far removed from their pioneer ancestry.

It is true. A sense of "struggle," and therefore "compassion," lingers in the sweet-smelling prairie air like a stubborn soldier of old, one who refuses to be stamped out by time or experience. And since nature reigns supreme, the people will watch, with a skeptical eye, anyone who tries to rise above the mystical forces governing the land and their way of life. You see, their ways are tried, tested, and true; they are trusted, revered, and loved. You can hear it in their voices, feel it in their warmth, see it in their actions. These people have not forgotten the wisdom of the old ways: They see merit in striking out on their own; they see value in staking a claim—no matter how small or seemingly insignificant.

For one thing, it is their way of dealing with the uncertainty of life; instead of sinking into a do-nothing mind-set, into a victim mentality, many of these people, in a carryover from the past, still like to make their very own mark on the world.

Of grandiose proportions, probably not. Of stupendous ramifications, possibly.

You see, this "can do" spirit keeps these people charged with enthusiasm for life, ready and willing to take on the next challenge. As if they thrive on adversity, when things go awry, prairie folks (most of them anyway) quickly pick themselves up, dust themselves off, and push on. As one gentleman puts it: "I can't stand to be burnin' daylight."

Our pioneer woman, Frances Nickel Jones, shares this story.

Back in 1923, I became ill when we lived in the log house. I was taken to the hospital; I had pneumonia in both lungs. I was in the hospital more than four months, flat on my back in bed for more than three of those months. Two or three times, I was not expected to live. My boys were six and eight years old. I worried about them constantly for fear they would be bitten by a rattlesnake or harmed by some accident. Yet I could not see them or do anything to help. They only got to town to see me one time. My husband was so busy trying to take care of the ranch work, the boys had to take care of themselves most of the time. I prayed day and night to God to take care of my boys and to help me get well so I could go home and take care of them and help with other things.

But then she goes on to say that her sons were "good boys," that the years spent on the prairie were "good years. They taught me many things I would never have known, like patience and trying to help others in any way I can."

At a crisp 104, we met Frances in an earlier chapter; she truly lights the way for those who are timid or fearful of meeting up with difficult times. Her charm, confidence, and emotional strength speak volumes about the value of knowing who you are and where you are going: Like an invisible anchor, this pioneer woman's ability to keep fighting back served her well. And she, like many other kindred spirits, helps preserve the endearing prairie spirit. Even today, when the value of striking out on one's own is minimized in favor of the "safe" course, the path of easiest resistance.

Unlike the sturdy prairie flowers, we seem to have forgotten the importance of valor in our lives, and even though most of us have the pluck to think and act independently, even when risky or ill-advised, how often do we exercise this option? How often do we follow our hearts into the wilderness of our souls, into the vast unknown of our ever so unique internal landscapes?

Surely as vast as the prairie itself, as the high-powered prairie sky, if not more so, we shun our interior worlds in exchange for showy exteriors made of disposable products: a safer route, of course; an easier reality, most assuredly; a less confounding perspective from which to view life, from which to puzzle our way through, certainly. Yet we miss so much. Like turning our back on a perfectly splendid sunset, walking through a lovely summer garden with our eyes shut tight, or entering a bakery with a gunnysack wrapped around our head, we close ourselves off to the best life has to offer.

I am reminded of the comments of Robert Adams, a retired astronomer, in *South Dakota Magazine*: "Fortunately, here in South Dakota . . . we may still enjoy such things as the subtle colors of dusk where the marriage of light and darkness produce the offspring of quiet beauty and peace." He adds: "In few places does the universe open its arms to the sensitive observer in such welcome." Yet how often do we fail to notice, to look, with all our senses tuned in, to the stunning beauty that beckons overhead and within each of us? The remedy: Choose a path requiring courage and heart; strike out on your own! It will open your eyes—to life, to yourself.

I've taken my fun where I've found it.

—RUDYARD KIPLING,

The Ladies

KICK UP YOUR HEELS

Do you ever think about the role of fun in your life? Do you squeeze it in around the edges like the last-minute cuff link, the almost forgotten birthday card to Great-aunt Sally, the hurried phone call to a distant friend? Or is it the frosting on the cake, the best part? Even then, do you ever feel guilty consuming "all that frosting," knowing you are eating the cake just so you can enjoy the sugary, sweet layer (your favorite flavor, of course) gracing the smooth top? Please don't panic, no confessions necessary.

These questions, rhetorical to be sure, only set the stage for a look at life, scanning for fun, for bits and pieces of time spent enjoying the moment, relishing the activity or the companionship that makes you smile, relax, or simply feel happy. Because it seems to me, as I consider the lifestyles and proclivities of people, institutions, and organizations, that we have come to downplay the importance of building fun into our twenty-first-century lives. Maybe, on a deeper level, we have forgotten how to have fun.

Consider your priorities for a minute. Where does fun appear— near the top, or quite near the bottom of your list? Is it there at all?

Quite possibly you equate it with something expensive or frivolous, even impossible; maybe fun, to you, is only to be experienced when all of the serious aspects of life have been taken care of first. I have met people who felt they had to keep a "lid" on having fun for fear it would come to dominate their time and life.

After all, we are taught the importance and considerable merit of responsibility from a very young age; we are told, ad infinitum: "Get your work done *first*, then play." So we come to segregate our lives into work and play and a constant tug-of-war emerges; eventually, many of us give up completely, removing "fun" from our list of priorities all together. And then we rush to justify our choice, if we are even aware of making it, by scornfully considering the lives of those around us (the minority, to be sure) who seem intent on having fun no matter what.

Do we not envy them really? Their ability to keep worries and responsibilities at bay or at least in perspective, when we have become slaves to our overly serious sides: to the things in life that are *supposed* to bring us happiness. But do these "things" ever deliver to the extent we expect or are we met instead with nameless feelings of discontent?

John Chaffee, Ph.D., author of *The Thinker's Way: 8 Steps to a Richer Life*, comments on the meaninglessness of our age, pointing out that: "We are too busy 'living' to wonder *why* we are living or who is doing the living. But can we afford to be too busy to find meaning in our lives?" he asks, suggesting in response that: "Our lives depend on the answer to this question. Not our biological lives necessarily, but the life of our *spirit*."

Chaffee goes on to quote theologian Paul Tillich, stressing his belief that we need the "courage to be" to create a life of meaning and purpose that is *individually* significant. Yet how can we create such a life when we rule out the wisdom of old ways, prairie-wise notions of those who lead meaningful lives based on simple, soulful concepts put into practice as a matter of course? We have become so "smart," we *think*;

we have become so "sophisticated" in our choices; and yes, we believe we have become so unlike those who preceded us. It is truly uncanny, our ability to deceive ourselves with such "lost-in-space" thinking.

Look at it this way: Some have even managed to convince themselves that they don't need "fun" in their lives anymore, that they are too busy, too polished, too broke, too bored by it all, too mature and rational to engage in something our children and grandchildren thrive on. And they tell themselves, like a parent tells a child, that they can get by without such silly diversions, pushing on in a relentless pursuit of something called "success."

I have to agree with John Chaffee when I ask: What in the world are we thinking? Or, are we thinking at all? So taken in by our own sense of importance, our feelings of infallibility and false confidence, we quite willingly settle for a meaningless existence over one that offers life.

PRAIRIE FUN

Not sure where or when the saying "kick up your heels" came to be, I recall hearing this phrase quite frequently as a young person growing up in the middle of nowhere. In other words: *Have some fun.* While this phrase is used in other parts of the country as well, for some reason I associate it with the days of the wild West, the cowboy era. Cowboy boots have heels, I guess, or some such logic as this. Fun, in those days, seemed to be built into the culture—almost unnoticeably at that; fun was the frosting on the cake, but it was also part and parcel of the cake itself. Having experienced different parts of the country, and as an avid observer of societal trends and transformations continually "at work," I have detected what I call the darkening, or muting, of the American psyche in that we seem to have lost touch with our ability to laugh at ourselves, to allow for mistakes and related good humor. And in so doing, we no longer build "fun" into our days, into our work.

With so much pressure to perform—no matter what our occupational status or personal situation—our focus has narrowed, while our hearts and souls have shriveled from neglect and worry. Consider the national crime rate, increased competition for rewarding careers, part-time parents who simply cannot get it all done, crowded classrooms with underpaid teachers, movies and books filled with violence and dissension, shifting or sinking values, a moral maze, misguided priorities, a burgeoning population, superficial lifestyles that alienate and divide.

Where is the balance? Where is the joyful dance of laughter between like-minded souls? Where is our ability to interject a sense of poetry into our harried lives?

Certainly there are exceptions, plenty of them, yet every society has an "essence," a core that radiates its most compelling aspects and properties. And with the plethora of self-help books on the market, the increasing number of "where-have-we-gone-wrong" type programs (TV, radio, private counselors), it is amazingly apparent that, as a nation, we feel shaky and uncertain and disenchanted. Newspaper headlines remind us of this on a very black-and-white level, but more important, we seem to know we have lost our way . . . to a point. Yet we seem unable to help ourselves, to look into our hearts and souls for answers. Curiously overwhelmed by the enormity of the task, we remain frozen and fearful as we passively wait for something—anything—to impact on the status quo in a positive fashion.

On the prairie, however, where people somehow keep their sights within "mortal limits," it is no wonder that, despite it all—harsh weather, limited economic opportunity, outsiders who callously advocate turning the area into a giant zoo and theme park (Buffalo Commons or some such thing) or maybe a landfill for waste disposal, modest to low income levels per capita, cultural tensions of old, and snide comments from those who look down on prairie residents as somehow "less" than those who live elsewhere—people just keep on having fun. No matter what.

Many seem to do this by keeping a healthy and positive sense of perspective, by truly valuing what they have—even though others, mostly outsiders, insist on knocking it—and by not being overly influenced by what goes on around them in terms of global events.

Consider this insightful commentary by Josh Holland of Tabor, South Dakota. At sixteen, as a junior in high school, Holland was asked to describe the state's strengths and shortcomings for an article in *South Dakota Magazine*. His words are memorable.

In 1989 Newsweek *depicted South Dakota of the future as a giant zoo and theme park, and as a new frontier for waste disposal. I was a fifth-grader then, intent on putting the magazine in its place as well as any ten-year-old could, so I joined with some friends to write a letter to the editor.* Newsweek *didn't publish it, but the editor sent us a letter of apology. Seven years later, I haven't forgotten that article. Who would dare think of turning this state into a landfill after seeing a Black Hills sunset? How could you turn South Dakota's heritage and tradition into a "Pirates of the Caribbean" experience? Nothing contrived can capture the essence of this place.*

I think of South Dakota as a stone among stones. It's too easy to think of certain other states as gems. Once California was golden; now many people there think of it as pyrite. To me South Dakota is a geode, plain at first glance, but filled with a multitude of dazzling facets.

At sixteen, Josh seemed to understand more about life than many adults do; he was able to put his feelings into words that anyone could appreciate; he was able to grasp the significance of the prairie—its timeless value, its inspirational spirit, its nonconforming ways—in a clear and determined manner. You have to admire his spunk, his ability to defend his home, the state, and place, he obviously loves.

Typical of prairie dwellers, a feisty attitude is indeed a desirable trait; it often conceals a great happiness, a knowing heart, a true kindness, a secret. No matter what others, "outsiders," do or say to minimize or reduce the prairie and her people, this confident group will go on doing what they have always done. Not into jumping through myriad hoops to please the outside world, prairie folks simply try to please themselves. And in doing this, they have learned not to take things too seriously. It would hurt too much, making them bitter and resentful; it would surely cause them to quit having fun!

So even though it may be disguised as hard work or may be masquerading as an everyday activity built into the day in a seamless, almost invisible, fashion, fun comes in many shapes and sizes on the prairie. Its role, important and life enhancing, has not been forgotten or supplanted by executive privilege, nor has it been replaced by high-dollar events and products. Clearly, it has not turned into something that only looks the part.

A SENSE OF ADVENTURE

On remote stretches of land, people have learned to turn mundane tasks and limited resources into something more. Sure, it takes some imagination, a willing heart, and a belief in simple, down-to-earth expectations, but having fun is a state of mind as much as anything, something undertaken to nourish the soul, to round out the rough edges life has a way of creating.

Very little is prepackaged on the prairie, however, so fun often requires a strong sense of imagination and adventure; it may require true respect for the healing power of humor, general goodwill, and the emotional bonding that can derive from sharing laughter with others. From the low-key picnic to the Sunday drive in the country, or maybe it is the high school rodeo, hunting prairie dogs, or a potluck wedding shower, fun is truly what you make it on the prairie.

And even though these people often work long, hard days—especially farmers and ranchers—that does not mean there is no time for fun. Rather, they simply build it into the project of the day whether that means branding cattle, putting up hay, harvesting wheat, canning pickled beets, watering the garden, or heading off to an office.

You see, even if it means taking time at lunch to throw a few horseshoes, play a quick hand of poker, or linger for a few jokes when the workday is over, there is little room for disappointment because expectations are kept on the realistic side. Here's what a few prairie experts say:

"Fun to me is not what a lot of other folks would call fun. I like to see something gained—to me, that is fun. To be friendly and have friends, and any work activity that turned out well."

"Fun is anything that makes me laugh. When the people one works with take the time to laugh and joke about things, any work activity becomes enjoyable."

"Fun is work that you enjoy."

A carryover from the days of the settlers, perhaps, this idea that fun does not have to be neatly segregated from "work" or ignored in the pursuit of loftier goals is captured by Laura Ingalls Wilder: "The American pioneer spirit (is) of courage, jollity, and neighborly helpfulness."

So when you get a chance to visit the prairie, leave your fancy duds at home; you won't need them at all, nor will you need to wait in a long line to buy a ticket to a sophisticated musical production. You will not need to plan far in advance, either, or make sure you are keeping up with your neighbors in terms of entertainment; you might want to bring your camera, however.

Nature walks are on the prairie menu, along with looking skyward to catch colorful sunsets that burn in your memory like a first kiss. Fishing may very well be in order, or making jelly with a neighbor, or maybe a church group is forming a softball team; and sometimes the best fun of all is simple conversation—casually joining with others to discuss the weather, the crops, the kids, the politics of the day, the newcomer from out East, the passing of a longtime friend, the birth of a child.

As long as there are people and prairie, there will be ample opportunities for fun because *real* fun dwells in the heart and soul just waiting for an excuse to show itself.

Everything an Indian does is in a circle,
and that is because the power of the world always works in circles,
and everything tries to be round.

—JOHN G. NEIHARDT,
Black Elk Speaks, Being the Life Story of a Holy Man
of the Ogalala Sioux

✑

GET YOUR WAGONS
IN A CIRCLE

It never ceases to amaze me: We know nothing happens in isolation, that the world has a rhythm and a rhyme of its very own, that everything is somehow connected, yet, without fail, we squirm against this reality like a new puppy on its first leash. We want to believe in our omnipotence; we want to conceal our natural and undeniable vulnerability; most assuredly, we want to downplay the significance of forces we cannot see. But don't we set ourselves up, albeit knowingly and willingly? By straining to live in opposition to a fundamental and universal law, we make things more difficult than they need be: Going against the grain, the natural direction, in most situations creates an underlying friction.

At times this can actually be a positive force—something needed to stimulate change. More often than not, however, our reluctance to acknowledge the interdependence of all living creatures, the unpredictable intertwining of events and unexplained happenings, adds to our stress level and general level of frustration. We spin our wheels, wondering why so little progress is made.

Worse yet, we exert precious energy and waste time blaming politicians, in-laws, the media, and the weather in an effort to "isolate" and define problems. Never bothering to look at the interrelationship between situations and circumstances and people, we ignore commonsense solutions in favor of simplistic reasoning based on our need to arbitrarily segregate good and evil, black and white—all because we do not like complexity. As a society, we seem to gravitate toward finger pointing and easy explanations requiring little of us on an emotional, spiritual, or intellectual level.

Some days I feel like we have truly lost our ability to "try," to look for win-win solutions, to address critical problems from a fresh and novel perspective. In many contexts, people have given up; they no longer look for a "better way" at all. Where is their pioneer spirit, their courage, their willingness to *try*?

Growing up on the very heart of the prairie, however, with a constant visual reminder of the omnipotence of nature—grasses swaying back and forth in perfect time, much like a metronome; a sky that welcomes, protects, inspires, and sometimes explodes; nighttime stars dotting the black heavens like a sea of diamonds; wide-open prairie needing nothing more than itself to make its mark on the world—something seemed to nudge me to view things differently. Gently so.

With compassion and quiet strength, the steadfast ardor of the magnanimous prairie spirit suggested a path with greater dignity and grace, one that encompasses instead of excluding, one that unites instead of pulling apart, one that appreciates the connectedness of people and place and time, not the disparities. I had been put in my place then and forever more. My life was not a meaningless string of random events to juggle, to divide and arrange at will, but a reflection of something greater, something that was only *part* of a much larger stage harboring unknown dimensions.

Certainly, the prairie, as a rule, forces us inward; according to Kathleen Norris, "by the sparseness of what is outward and visible in all this land and sky." But the prairie had also forced me "outward" by calling to my immediate attention the vastness of nature—of things that are bigger and broader than any individual—the panoramic view, a vantage point that included everyone and everything without picking and choosing on an arbitrary basis. Wonderfully freeing, this sort of perspective encouraged me to appreciate the very human qualities in everyone while not expecting perfection or distinction or comparisons (often ugly, unfair, and needless) that, curiously, seemed to make the world go round.

For one thing, it felt unkind. For another, it seemed mildly destructive. And finally, such useless "me against you" thinking seemed unsophisticated and self-indulgent; it also seemed downright negative, unholy, and, certainly, careless: People—human beings—should not be judged so harshly, so swiftly. Who are *we* to judge? Why are we so eager to pass judgment on others, on their intentions, as if we, mere mortals, are godlike?

Aren't we all in this together—this thing called life? And if any aspect of our earthly experience can be improved, aren't we all better off, really?

These were my thoughts growing up on the prairie in the fifties, sixties, and seventies; and even though I asked more questions than I ever dreamed would be answered, my deepest convictions grew from these mental meanderings. Of course I have continued to ponder life ever since (how could I not?), and at times I have also strayed from my prairie roots in search of a different reality, only to grow dissatisfied and curiously circumspect about voicing my beliefs.

Not everyone agreed.

CONNECT THE DOTS

Still, to this day I envision a world where people recognize the importance of multiple roles, of working harmoniously together to create a marvelous whole, where mending fences and caring about all human beings is more important than burning bridges. And since the most basic of pictures is not complete until all the pieces connect, until the total image is formed, there is a certain amount of prairie wisdom in considering the big picture while we have an opportunity to have a significant impact: Life and death inevitably come full circle, too, or like a genuine cowboy might put it: "As sure as shootin' we're all gonna kick the bucket."

This topic is not mentioned to be morbid or overly somber; nor is it a prairie pastime to spend an inordinate amount of time thinking about death.

Rather, to better understand the circular design of the world, to live and work and love within a framework of mystical yet predictable design, there is value in examining the final, culminating event from a prairie perspective. Among the people—and remember, this is not a culture marked by youth, fancy cars, expensive clothes, or flashing lights—death is truly part of life. Not in a detached, wringing-of-the-hands sense; rather, death exists in a pure context of ultimate surrender to the land, to the place that invites quiet contemplation concerning the truths of our existence, the mystery of life and death.

Formed of the past and sustained by the present, the prairie culture I know and value is rich, warm, and real. Without pretense, undue complication, or weighty expectations, the prairie simply presents itself: unadorned beauty conveying power that is personal and dynamic in every way.

How refreshing! How inviting! How peaceful yet invigorating! How captivating, inspiring, and compelling! And yes, how utterly distinctive.

All of this and more, the prairie and its people, even today, radiate completeness: life and death, then and now, black and white. And in seeking nothing more, in its very openness to providing a special place of quiet, natural dimensions, the land offers a final resting place without comment or fanfare. Linked to beginnings of remarkable stride, while eagerly supporting growth and longevity, the prairie also invites its inhabitants to sleep peacefully when the last breath is taken.

Come home, day is done.

THE CIRCLE OF LIFE

What part of the universal circle does your life, indeed, your soul, represent? What aspects of your immediate life circle does your heart wrap itself around—protectingly, lovingly, joyfully? How many "circles" does your life have an impact on? Are they distant, of moderate proximity, close, or intimate?

Maybe you have never thought about your life in those terms. But in the end, it is the "circle of life" that draws us close, keeping us focused on what is meaningful. On what is truly true.

Try to envision a circle of life-sustaining covered wagons, white but dust covered and almost touching: one to one, in a snug, tightly held ring. A shield against the forces that be, seen and unseen, a symbol of unity, a perfect reflection of the pioneer spirit, a source of power, love, and fortitude—all of this and more marked the appearance of wagon trains come to rest in a traditional circle at nightfall when the prairie lands grew dark and mysterious. Have things really changed since the mid to late 1800s? Since the era of covered wagons slowly rolled across the rough prairie ground in search of opportunity and freedom, an inspirational domain offering new life? Most people, still today, are in search of something they do not quite understand; and at night, when cool breezes filter in and around the campfire, when the heavens turn dark yet splendid with an actual peek into infinity, we gather our circle of friends and loved ones together, for warmth and protection and inspiration as we reflect on the day, as we restore our spirits for the next day, as we faithfully wait for the dawn.

Hear the words of O. E. Rölvaag in his opening chapter, "Toward the Sunset," from *Giants in the Earth*, first published in 1927.

It was late afternoon. A small caravan was pushing its way through the tall grass. The track it left behind was like the wake of a boat—except that instead of widening out astern it closed in again. . . . The caravan seemed miserably frail . . . as it crept over the boundless prairie toward the sky line. Of road or trail there lay not a trace ahead. . . . Poverty-stricken, unspeakably forlorn, the caravan creaked along, advancing at a snail's pace, deeper and deeper into a bluish-green infinity. . . .

On and on they went, farther out toward Sunset Land—farther into the deep glow of the evening. . . . At the moment when the sun closed his eye, the vastness of the plain seemed to rise up on every hand—and suddenly the landscape had grown desolate; something bleak and cold had come into the silence, filling it with terror. . . . Behind them, along the way they had come, the plain lay dark green and lifeless, under the gathering shadow of the dim, purple sky.

Ole sat motionless at his mother's side. The falling of evening had made such a deep impression on him that his throat felt dry; he wanted to express some of the emotions that overwhelmed him, but only choked when he tried. . . . The sombre blue haze was now closing rapidly in on the caravan. One sensed the night near at hand; it breathed a chill as it came. . . .

But now something seemed to be brewing back there over the prairie whence they had come. Up from the horizon swelled a supernatural light—

a glow of pale yellow and transparent green, mingled with strange touches
of red and gold. It spread upward as they watched; the colors deepened;
the glow grew stronger, like the witching light of a fen fire.

Surely you can sense the prairie's incredible power in his words. How it can provoke, subdue, and overwhelm, how it can encourage us to draw close against the night. How it propels us inward, shivering, wondering, praying for the gods to look kindly on us. Quite simply, a stunning, sometimes quivering body of land destined to have an impact on mankind in ways only history and our modern-day imaginations can reveal.

And so it is that we speak of the prairie today at the dawn of the twenty-first century.

KNOWLEDGE COMES, WISDOM LINGERS

Another circular construct bearing meaning and dignity for nearly everyone—treasured family relationships, especially those between young and old. From Singapore to Alaska to the prairie lands, their unique configurations buoy our lives in innumerable ways. But when was the last time you tried to put yourself in an aging relative's shoes? I recall my grandmother's old age with a mixture of sadness and joy—such a wonderful human being, a work of art, a personal treasure beyond anything I had known. Yet I knew she wouldn't be with us forever; she knew it, too.

Looking back, I wonder if we were truly sensitive to that simple fact, or did we dance around the inevitable out of a basic discomfort with our emotions? Did we fail to honor the fear, the impending sense of loss and finality, that had quietly wrapped itself around our interactions with her? Like a brilliant moon in a darkened sky, the light of her soul captured our hearts, touched our souls with something nameless, almost primitive, yet we seemed to lack the courage to say: "Thank you." For all she had done, for all she had given us, for her knowledge, her considerable wisdom, for showing us how to live, for teaching us the importance of truth, kindness, and concern. Yes, we told her of our love; we hugged her and smiled, and she would smile back, too, then wink—even at ninety-eight—as if she were sharing many secrets with us.

A woman of the prairie, having lived a long life without luxuries, fanfare, or pretense, having never even driven an automobile, she radiated a sense of perfection, peace, and utter completeness; it should have prompted us to thank her for sharing her life with us, simple words with such incredible power. I guess we thought she knew; I guess we didn't stop to think about the obvious, about how much those words might have meant to her.

Yet saying thank you is such a wonderful acknowledgment of another person's role in your life—your success, your defeats and hard times, your joys. Two words that readily sum up the circular nature of relationships and life, they indicate respect, caring, appreciation, and, ultimately, equality, understanding, and empathy. What could be more important to share with someone you have loved, someone who is facing the end of life as we know it?

Very little. But we shy away from it in this context because those everyday words force us to come to terms with reality: A loved one is about to complete his or her circle of life. Painful, yes, so we make small talk to avoid talking about the things that matter, the things we need and want to say. We chicken out. Yet I look at the personal story of Frances Nickel Jones, the courageous woman introduced early in the book, and at 104, she begins eight pages of handwritten notes like this: "Dear

Friend Daisy, Thank you for this opportunity to help you, if I can with your book—I do wish you success."

Then she goes on to tell me about her years in a log house on the prairie in the early 1900s: that she was born in Illinois in 1895, that her mother died in 1905, and that her father, feeling unable to care for the three children, placed them in separate foster homes. The family she was placed with moved to South Dakota in 1909. Meanwhile, her father married again: "He and his wife had seven more children. I am the oldest of all of the ten children—and today I am the only one of the ten children left. I guess South Dakota has been a good place for me to live."

Frances recalls being at her mother's bedside as a young girl (ten years old) when she died: "That was a hard thing for me to do—then I lost my first baby boy during childbirth—then in 1928 I lost my first husband because of a stroke. I lost my second husband in 1972. During these years I lost my brother and my seven half-sisters and brothers. I lost my oldest son, Louie, in 1995. He had cancer. In 1997 I lost my ninety-five-year-old sister. The hardest of all of these to part with was my son—I still miss him so much—he was so good to me. It is hard for a mother to give up her children." She closes with these words:

"If you can get any help from this letter or the answers to your questions, then I'm glad—With love, Frances Nickel Jones." To honor her wonderful, life-giving spirit, I say: *Thank you*, Frances, for sharing your life with us in this book of prairie wisdom.

Most of us will not endure what she has; most of us will not reach 104; and clearly, most of us will not have such a humble and knowing heart, one that is so obviously filled with love and regard for others. As a source of inspiration, as a vision of what we are all capable of in our finer, more understanding and humane moments, may her lovely spirit, her graceful walk through life guide us in our search for a road map to the heart.

For the power of the heart should not be underestimated in our lives. Few compasses guide us more accurately to the places, beliefs, and people who matter, to the practices and values that would keep our world safe and hospitable for all living creatures, to the connections that help us sustain the ever important circle of life.

THE POWER OF HOME

Well-known statistics reveal the extent to which people move around— to a new city, a new country perhaps, to a new home within the same town. Opportunities for change abound. Living our lives "away from our home" as so many do has created pockets of discontent within society, fragments of "circles" dotting the landscape. There is a wistful quality to our world, apparent in people's voices, faces, and dreams—acknowl- edged and vice versa. "Something is missing" floats in the air, eerily mingling with smiling crowds, hovering just beyond our consciousness like an especially poignant memory, one we cannot seem to forget.

Clearly, I cannot speak for everyone, but, for me at least, the missing piece is home: my place of birth and growing-up years. For me, the prairie. When cut off from this place for too long, I feel incomplete, even melancholy at times. And though writing about my homeland has been quite enjoyable, sharing it with people the world over—a great honor—it is not the same as being there face-to-face. I do not believe I am unique in this regard, because I know people who also live away from their roots; it is nearly always a mixed blessing leaving pieces of circles floating here and there—leaving our hearts wide open, searching for meaningful connections to replace the ones we have lost.

It is somewhat like what I read in a tiny book about the practice of Zen, wherein the author, Charlotte Joko Beck, suggests that if she were to scratch the surface of any one person she would find anxiety, fear, and pain running amok. And since each of us comprise the world, in the collective sense, imagine the totality of those feelings on the psyche of the world, on us. A "friendly" face can hide only so much; a "friendly" world can hide only so much: The undercurrent of anything can be very strong indeed.

If a portion of your internal pain stems from a feeling of being disconnected from your roots, go home. Share your childhood memories with your friends, your children and grandchildren. Close the circle, make it complete, whenever possible. If your current existence does not feel right or real, then as the book title suggests, *Look Homeward, Angel.* Not without its own set of problems, limitations, or complications, going home can be a rewarding experience. It works for me.

Whether for a short vacation or for more extended stays (in the early nineties, I returned to South Dakota for four years), there is no clearer reference point for who we are and what we are all about than home. As Black Elk points out in the chapter's opening quote, power always works in circles. Also true of "personal power," time at home, close to your roots, can help you reclaim your sense of personal power, inspiring you onward, lighting your way for the journey that remains with renewed strength, energy, and focus.

I had to wonder why, in the middle
of the South Dakota prairie,
Who in their right mind would start
a damn dairy.

— BARRY TYLER,
"In Loving Memory of A. B. Tyler, 1999"

༄

EMBRACE THE PAST

Good, bad, or in-between, the past, your past, my past, *our* past informs the present and the future. Yet evidence of what came before us, clearly all around us, often seems overshadowed by the pressures, pains, and pleasures of the moment. And so it is that we fail to embrace the past— that which instructs, supports, reveals, and prepares us for today and tomorrow. Fortunately, the force of history is insistent.

The past seeks to be duly recognized and understood, and even when it seems to all but shout at us, we often turn away—a bit too eagerly, a bit too energetically. Are we afraid of what the past represents, of what there is to know, to consider and contemplate?

Or does bringing the past into our lives in some meaningful way simply make us feel unsuitably dressed, like attending a formal event in all the wrong clothes, or like walking in late, just as everyone is leaving? Nobody wants to feel out of step with the times, nor do we want to feel stuck in the past, forced to watch the rest of the world go by. As the lyrics to a song go, "Your life is now."

But what happens, with amazing predictability, when we attempt to ignore something or someone? Something important, relevant, and perhaps meant to be; someone who wants, needs, and depends on our attention, affection, and interest? Whatever or whomever it is becomes increasingly insistent and impatient, unusually loud, and strangely constant, until we acknowledge the person, place, or thing calling out to us, until we stop to pay attention. As some would say, until we stop to smell the roses or pick the daisies, whatever your preference may be.

On a friend of mine's T-shirt, a favorite, is this: "Climb More Mountains; Read More Books; Eat More Ice Cream; Pick More Daisies." So there you have it: The choice is yours, as long as the implication, the essence of the idea or activity, remains true to its fundamental mission.

Do the things that beg for your attention, that which you routinely put off as too distant, too long ago, too unusual, too much bother, too difficult, too impractical, too wild and weird, too obvious and common-place, too much fun. And if something from your past is nagging at you, like a pesty but well-meaning friend, give in: Go exploring, see what there is to see. Pulled in one direction or another, usually for a reason, it can be tempting to overlook the past in our mad rush to go forward, even more tempting to minimize the importance of understanding, ac-cepting, and embracing the past with all its many imperfections and missteps. Yet its force is real; it pulses through your heart and soul with a life of its own. And by making it yours, instead of ignoring or discred-iting it, you actually bring things into balance and perspective; the past no longer holds such great power over you—your present or your future. By turning to face the past head on, there is much to be gained. You discover how much you have changed, how much growth you have ex-perienced along the way. In essence, by comparing your former self with who you are today, it is possible to appreciate your evolving identity with a certain amount of satisfaction. It can be truly eye-opening.

On the South Dakota prairie, where the past feels as vital as the present (the mix is truly captivating), where these lessons are oh so clear, old barns, churches, historical markers, mature cottonwoods, and meadowlarks, which don't compete with anything but vast stretches of graceful, ever present prairie and sky, announce their survival, indeed, their special prominence, with an air of timelessness. In contrast, we are encouraged to consider our own existence, the very fact that we have a finite length of time in which to fulfill our dreams. To share, learn, and grow. To fall down and pick ourselves up again.

To let our hearts and souls experience the depths of despair, the beauty and rapture of relationships only a divine power could design, the perfect peace of a starlit prairie sky.

And so we are met with a choice: to let our lives slip through our fingers like a ghostly image of short, unknown duration, or to choose to listen to the prairie wind, to its wise counsel, by embracing life in all its many dimensions—past, present, future—while the time is ours and ours alone.

Since the prairie represents a rather infinite time sequence, its message is clearly one of precision: Amid priceless simplicity and an unchanging, unwavering ability to inspire and involve and encourage even the dreariest, most despondent inhabitant, the prairie gently reminds us by its mere presence, its spirit, that life is not something to be taken lightly, or worse yet, for granted.

Our connection to a larger purpose is quite clear when living or standing within the prairie's sphere—a humbling experience that greatly enlarges the idea of "roots." More than a family name, a place, or a group of people who have been part of your world for a long time, having prairie roots means being connected to the past in a very visible and powerful way. And by encouraging you to think well beyond your lifetime, to look over your shoulder and down the road a bit as well, you are able to enlarge your sense of place, and, ultimately, your sense of purpose.

KEEPING US WHOLE

What about our memories, the wondrous role they play in our daily lives? Not a day goes by when we don't recall something from our childhood or growing-up years, when we don't have a few special moments come to mind from almost out of the blue. A bit like the "past in action," our remembrances offer us clever and worthwhile information: We are reminded of strengths and weaknesses, of when things fell apart or mysteriously came together, of times when something made us laugh or cry or simply lose our cool.

In short, memories give us an automatic reference point for situations and people encountered in the present, but they also give us an ongoing guide to the future as well.

Our past, in the form of all-important memories, is like an internal library filled with volumes of topics: life and death, relationships, career interests, hobbies, passions, and more. We also remember certain smells, certain places, and certain people with amazing clarity: Some memories stand out in our minds like they happened "just yesterday."

Then some are fuzzy; we can't quite make them out, even when we spend a significant amount of time trying to produce, or re-create, the intriguing details of the moment. And some memories are mere sensations, they have an ephemeral quality to them, while others float through our minds on a more constant basis, like the backdrop on a stage, usually noticed, yet primarily part of the overall picture. The sky of your life in a way.

Prairie memories, those thoughts, feelings, and internal records that locals compile throughout a lifetime, include the lifelike feel of the land. Indeed, it is the backdrop of their lives, the living "memory" that sets the stage for daily life in all its many forms and adaptations. Sometimes it feels this way—that if you look right over the next hill, you might see a sod shanty providing shelter for a pioneer family, a covered wagon, or at least a trail, or a few buffalo roaming free. Maybe Sitting Bull himself, quietly resting amidst the prairie landscape to consider life and his people.

And surely you will find, scattered here and there, a few lone campfire rings, now extinguished but bearing signs of life—the steady march forward into wide-open lands offering solitude and room to grow.

The past is truly that real on the prairie, so people naturally draw "yesterday" close to their hearts. How could they not? An ever present force, the prairie reminds and focuses us: It tells its story each day; it acts as a constant companion, one experienced in matters of the heart; it effectively bridges the gap between past and present and future, fusing them into a splendid whole. A quilt of many colors, a swirling design representing a gorgeous piece of art. The culture, as a whole, also represents the past: slow and reluctant and somehow impervious to change; vivid reminders of bad guys in black hats immortalized for their bad deeds; cowboys and cowgirls gearing up for the next rodeo.

By design and happenstance, it is all still there. And while this may seem rather inconsequential, the past can be a rich source of courage, inspiration, and vision. As one person put it after a lifetime on the prairie: "The past shows a person that if you have the will to succeed and do a good job, you can overcome most any obstacle." And this comes from someone who has indeed had to overcome a variety of obstacles. Yet his wiser instincts, his knowledge of self and life and love, led him to believe in the ultimate value of past experience: Hold it close to your heart, let it linger in a treasured place, *keep it with you,* unless, of course, it damages your sense of compassion or dignity, your heartfelt vision of what you and your life is all about.

Then it is right to let it go, move on to those new places that offer you peace, joy, and purpose of heart. The past is not meant to hold us captive when its path has grown dim or confining; nor will it hide us from the world for long.

OUR NATION'S PAST

We all have an immediate past, along with a more distant past reaching back to our days as an infant; but we also have a "built-in past," one that actually precedes our physical time on planet earth—ancestors who stretch back across the decades, the personal context of time gone by. And we have a shared history in terms of our nation's past. While we only experience a fraction of our "total" history, our lives represent nothing less than the cumulative effect of time itself, of all that has transpired since the birth of our civilization and our nation.

And so it is, at the turn of the century and beyond, that an excellent opportunity arises to consider our nation's past in relation to its present and certainly in terms of its future. More than a history lesson, definitely more than a few snapshots highlighting the highs and lows of an era, when looking through our prairie lens, polished and expertly positioned, we see so much more.

Time has been a tremendous teacher, one that we often underestimate in its legitimate appeal and ability to transform. Powerful, magical, poetic, and inspirational, the passage of time gives us an incredible gift: a second, third, fourth, or fifth chance, and thereby it gives us something even larger, something we seek in differing degrees at various points in our lives—freedom.

Somehow apparent from a prairie perspective, our nation's history, indeed, our world's history as reflected in the passage of time reveals, more than anything, a million and one mistakes. But, luckily, we have been granted a seemingly unlimited number of chances to do things differently, from a wiser, more knowing, outlook—we have picked up some prairie secrets along the way. As travelers in a journey we do not quite understand, as the past manifested in the present, as pioneers of the twenty-first century, we have learned that less is more. And in the context of embracing our nation's past, that actually means a good deal.

Some of our nation's "bigger" mistakes seem predicated on a formidable and ongoing need to overpower others, to consume and control without regard for the consequences, to dominate and direct "that and those" who display weakness or resistance.

Our nation's ability and desire to try and muscle its way through key situations is truly uncanny, but aggression is not always the answer: Less can indeed be more. By giving others room to express their individuality, to muddle through issues in an effort to chart their own special course, to let unique qualities shine through with vision and honor, we have much to gain. Most people will find their way through life if we have the good sense to let them. The path and choices may sometimes look strange; it may seem like there is no path at all, when, in fact, he or she may have chosen an "inspired" path, or a "learning" path, one without obvious distinction, understanding, or appeal.

So now, as our nation's journey takes us into a new millennium with no sign of covered wagons, sod shanties, or one-room schoolhouses dotting the prairie landscape, perhaps our challenge is this: to embrace the past—like it or not, it is our past; to heal the wounds of our time and the eras that preceded us; to celebrate meaningful progress; to take a penetrating look at our world and where it seems to be headed. And then if you do not sense a path with heart, if you feel ill at ease with the patterns in your life and with the world direction, and if there is a nagging little voice trying to tell you something—listen. The world's future is in your hands.

Happiness doesn't depend on what we have but it does depend
on how we feel towards what we have.
We can be happy with little and miserable with much.

—WILLIAM DEMPSTER HOARD,
AMERICAN PUBLISHER AND AGRICULTURIST

(1836–1918)

KEEP A SONG IN YOUR HEART

Machines, objects, and technology, draw reverence from us; human beings with admirable qualities draw mild or passing interest from us, some positive, some negative. Who is he to behave in such an outstanding manner, showing up the rest of us for the whole world to see? Or perhaps our skeptical nature takes over: What is she really up to?

While the dynamics of human behavior are never simple and some people really are up to something undesirable, it seems that we go out of our way to minimize or negate sentiments and actions that show true merit. Integrity, high standards, compassion, and intelligence do make their mark, and when noticed, these attributes apply a certain amount of pressure on the rest of us: Do we measure up? we quietly ask ourselves. Some even appear to harbor a curious need to sabotage the well-meaning efforts of such an individual.

And when someone is basically a "happy" person—she or he supports and encourages others; displays a generally positive, but realistic, attitude; takes an active interest in daily challenges and opportunities without getting bogged down or giving up; presents a warm, caring, open-minded style—look out. (While an excessive amount of cheer can annoy, here I am referring to a healthy level of goodness grounded in reality and thoughtfulness.) Happy people, often ridiculed or simply not taken seriously, seem to bug unhappy people to no end. An entire range of reasons, some legitimate, most nonsensical, come to mind; yet on the prairie, where culture, time, and place join forces to influence our thinking, to shed light on our misconceptions, there is clear evidence of the fundamental value of happiness.

A STATE OF MIND

Zero in on your state of mind: Are you someone who passes on good vibes and a smile, or are you a person who gets a strange sort of satisfaction, even pleasure, from the trials and tribulations of others, from the down side of life?

Or maybe you require an excessive amount of external stimulation, an inordinate degree of excitement to feel "happy." You firmly believe that life on the prairie, even today, would drive you absolutely berserk, causing you to feel downright bored, terribly *un*happy, frustrated, and adrift—like someone put out to pasture before her time.

And very well you might, especially if you are hooked on flashing lights, blaring sirens, constant stimulation, new this and new that, trends, fads, and entirely novel situations—nearly everything that contributes to the sensory overload of the twenty-first century: time compression (excessively demanding schedules more suitable to robots than human beings, which cause many to feel continually tense and rushed), an overabundance of material effects, a world economy that neither waits nor rests, a burgeoning population, a fast-paced global pulse that dictates the terms of our everyday life, a quickening of our minds to the point where our hearts and souls can barely keep up.

These trends all had a beginning, too; they do not represent entirely new phenomena. As noted by Robert Hopke in *There Are No Accidents: Synchronicity and the Stories of Our Lives*, "The sad fact of twentieth-century history is, as Einstein remarked, that the development of our technology has outstripped the development of our humanity to the extent that an unparalleled destruction of our human life was made possible in the form of the Holocaust. Not that mass destruction has not always been the shadow of human history. . . ."

Clearly, the Dakotas, and indeed, our nation, has not been immune to such problems—tides of senseless destruction stemming from an inability to honor and understand diversity, from the rationalization of abhorrent behavior, such as found in many institutional settings across America, where human beings are treated without a shred of dignity or concern.

But if technology was a problem then, imagine its effect on our world now. Perhaps in the end, preserving life as we know it will come down to this: our ability, as a species, to contain the negative effects of a burgeoning technology in relation to our survival.

One thing is certain, however, and this may seem relatively minor in comparison to the issues being addressed, but "happy" people did not cause the Holocaust. And while life on the prairie does not guarantee a happy state of mind, there is, at a minimum, a real opportunity to define and discover, from the inside out, what can realistically create and sustain true happiness.

Quietly forcing us to go beyond conventional, popularized thinking, which spells out and suggests a multitude of ways to "buy" happiness, the prairie, the place and its people, does not advocate specific, one-size-fits-all remedies. Rather, the emphasis, while often understated, can be found in the contrast between the "outside world" and the calm of another world—the prairie's world.

In a place where very little stands between an individual and his or her innermost self, the chances of a true encounter are greatly enhanced, and it thus becomes incumbent on a thinking person to do some soul-searching around the issue of happiness. Contemporary society, with its many bells and whistles, offers a different fare, and while it can create an image of abundance, its actual effect is often miragelike.

When genuine happiness, which endures beyond the moment and in spite of external events or things, is the goal, common sense reminds us of the need for an internal source to replenish our emotions, to sustain a state of mind cultivated and cared for much like a bountiful garden. Otherwise, we are at the complete mercy of what is happening around us and to us, and when it comes to feeling happy, what could be less satisfying, less meaningful?

Happiness can be a choice, something you grant yourself regardless of external circumstances, and it does not have to come with a steep price tag as is too often assumed. But you have to give yourself permission to be happy "despite it all," and you have to know how to cultivate a happy state of mind. It rarely falls in your lap.

My grandmother, who spent almost ninety-eight years living on and with the prairie, liked to put it this way: "Keep a song in your heart." And if I were to summarize her approach to life, the timeless guidance she unknowingly left behind through her actions, this is what gave her unlimited joy and happiness, this is what she would have told us at the dawn of the twenty-first century: Enjoy nature; tend to your chores; nurture plants, flowers, trees, and animals; appreciate the natural beauty and harvest of life; give away what you do not need; smile, laugh, and care;

and most of all, keep it simple. So while you must put effort into staying reasonably happy, the road, if filled with heart, is not incredibly daunting.

A CAPACITY TO LEARN

The prairie is not wont to change its ways. Day after day, month after month, the scene rarely, if ever, changes: Sameness rules. Like an anchor, the prairie setting stands still for us as we are born, live, and die.

Deep grasses, gentle breaks in the land, a wide-eyed sky—it is a comforting presence reflecting a magnanimous spirit, a happy heart. A living anchor yet a free spirit—one of the prairie's most appealing features. Truly, the land represents both vantage points, an interesting and intriguing paradox subject to much interpretation, one of the biggest reasons locals literally fall in love with the prairie, I think. And in pondering this dichotomy, I came to realize that the prairie, snow covered or dotted in wildflowers, even wearing its plain golden brown of summer and fall, has the power to make me feel happy. Quite happy, at that.

The prairie represents the perfect state of being (contained, stable, and firmly rooted yet primarily free of man-made influences); it reflects the "wholeness" of life on a level we will probably never experience. It appeals to our finer senses, teasing and playing with our imagination; most important, the prairie helps us to learn. In trying to solve its many mysteries, we grow smarter, sometimes wiser. Most certainly, we grow spiritually. And this kind of personal drama, dynamic and powerful, can also lead to happiness, because greater self-awareness is often liberating.

Then there is the strong sense of survival that the prairie offers:

Those who live there realize, with a certain sense of quiet accomplishment, that they are sturdy souls who have adapted and befriended a demanding land, one that challenges through its connection to nature, one that inspires through its natural beauty. But in making peace with the prairie, its power and its starknesss, again, feelings of happiness often bubble up to the surface.

So even as people of the land, insiders, newly arrived outsiders, or outsiders on their way to becoming insiders scurry through their daily routines, the prairie remains steadfast and certain, never wavering or turning away yet free to confound and confuse, free to live on its own terms.

Hopefully, we, as a free people, will have the wisdom in the coming years to preserve, honor, and cherish the prairie lands. They offer ample opportunity for self-discovery, and if our humanity is indeed to keep pace with our technology, even in the remotest sense, we will need all the self-awareness we can unearth.

Einstein was not far off in his assessment of the twentieth century; let us not continue down the same path in a vain attempt to forget the things we already know, in a futile effort to ignore basic human needs, like the need for happiness. Listen to the words of those who love the land; hear the reverence and joy the prairie evokes from them.

One South Dakota artist, Cherie Ramsdell, who is known for her unique raku pottery (the process was perfected in sixteenth-century Japan) uses her deep connection to the land to further inspire her artistry. When I asked her to describe the most beautiful aspect of prairie life, she offered the following: "To me, it is the ability to be an individual and truly alone for self-reflection. Also the constant reminder that there truly is a force larger than myself. If you question the existence of God all you need to do is lay on an empty prairie, listen, and look up." Ramsdell also says she has learned important things from prairie life: resiliency, the ability to adapt and innovate, the pure pleasure of hard work and accomplishment.

Mary Jewel Ledbetter, a prairie resident for more than seventy-eight years, put it this way: "The most beautiful aspect of prairie life is being wrapped around by nature." She adds, "The prairie teaches patience and perseverance, along with reverence for God's great world—we are part of it all, not masters of it." And finally, "I find deep peace when I am looking out over the prairies of western South Dakota. They are closer to heaven than any place on earth. The power of the rolling plains is hard to explain, but easy to feel. The ability to see for forty or fifty miles is exciting—nothing clutters your view!"

Other comments from longtime residents reveal similar sentiments. One prairie resident of 101 years, Mera Andresen, simply points out that nature works best; and our featured pioneer woman, Frances N. Jones, writes: "Most of the things on the prairie are beautiful in their natural state. Leave the prairie in its natural state as much as possible." Oh how her sensible words ring true. But are we smart enough to listen? Or will we turn away from the prairie's offerings—peace, solace, happiness, personal growth, inspiration, and self-knowledge—in our haste to "advance"?

As a new day dawns, remember, we are responsible for our own fate, for the fate of our children and grandchildren. So as you take the prairie's wisdom into your heart and soul, consider the words and ways of those who have traveled before you, because when the capacity to learn is lost, hope is also lost.

And when a people, indeed, a land or a country, is without hope, there can be no happiness, no meaningful way to survive and prosper.

Think about it.

There is no covered wagon for you to travel in, but there is new, unexplored territory just ahead. Let us remain open to learning, hopeful about our future, and dedicated to the challenges of our time. And may the pioneer spirit of old resonate within you as we chart our course, as steep and arduous as it may be, for there is no turning back.

Oh to dwell on the sweet past

Where most of my life is cast

A smile, a face, a time, a place,

There is so much to retrace.

Oh to walk that trail once more,

To redo the things I adore.

Misty eyed and with deep sigh,

I watch the reel of life go by.

—HAROLD H. SCHULER,

Pierre Since 1910

MAKE TIME FOR
THE IMPORTANT THINGS

Volumes have been written about time: how to manage it, control it, use it, beat it, indeed, how to have more of it; nowadays it is nearly impossible to stop thinking about time. Clocks, calendars, and computers remind us of deadlines, priorities, appointments, and schedules until we feel ready to explode. Yet no matter what formula we adopt, no matter what fad we embrace, nothing seems to change.

The world has become a place of frenzy and frantic pursuit in a number of significant contexts. "Hurry" has taken on new meaning, new urgency, and is often engrained in our minds at a young age, never to be forgotten, easily dismissed or countered. A friend of mine recently explained how "hurry" rattles through his mind almost continually, in the background of his thoughts like a never ending freight train rumbling down a winding track with no final destination at all.

We hurry, we rush, we forget to say no. At times we even run around in circles, not knowing where the circle began, where, or if, it will end. You know the feeling, I'm sure. As seen in previous chapvters, however, the prairie suggests a deeper, broader definition of time—one that moderates the exacting pressures of family, work, and society; one offering a strong sense of renewal. While everyone around us seems to be asking something of us, the gentle prairie lands seem to be *giving* us something. Wholeheartedly, too. Like a best friend who keeps your best interests at heart even when tempted to keep score.

The prairie perspective on time has rubbed off on the people who live there; for the most part they still take (and make) time for each other, so basic values and honest needs of a very "human" variety remain in the forefront, not the next deadline, company meeting, country club function, or shopping spree. While such things may be important, the prairie culture refuses to be controlled by anything other than the simple and honest ways of the heart.

The people somehow sense the need to honor the human elements, giving those areas priority over things that can, if necessary, wait. In a place where continuity and quiet compassion predominate, the dividing line emerges naturally, almost magically, and from this sensitive stance, it is easier to keep egos in line, the environment, for the most part, being calmer, less rushed and impulsive and crazed with "go-here-now, be-there-now" type sentiments.

Since there will never be enough time, no matter who does the scheduling, no matter where you reside or what you do to make your life meaningful and purposeful, the culture, indeed the people who comprise it, does not make unreasonable demands, nor does it force everyone to move at the same pace. Where nature calls the shots, people are less insistent about getting their way. Where caring for animals and crops often takes center stage, again, most people have come to accept delays, emergencies, and prairie priorities with a certain amount of aplomb. You really get the feeling in talking to these people, those who grew up with the land and the sky at their side, that it would take something major, something difficult to even envision, to rattle them.

Too many roaring blizzards when livestock needlessly lost their lives, or too many dry summers when crops struggled each day just to survive, too many windy days when the dust blew free with a life of its very own. These factors have taken their toll, on these people, on this place, where the only sure thing in life is a strong and caring heart.

Thus, rushing around in a senseless battle to get everything done in just the right order does not appeal to them. Most people have strong beliefs about what's important, what's not, so making time for the important things comes naturally; and the bottom line is this: if their heart is not in something, it probably won't get done, or not quickly, anyway.

CAPTAIN OF YOUR SHIP

When was the last time you thought about your personal priorities besides when you read the previous chapter on "fun"? Does the outside world control your day, your night, your entire agenda, week to week, month to month, year to year? Are you in a reactionary mode a great deal when you would prefer to be acting on your own needs and inclinations, at least some of the time? Maybe the important things are buried in an overwhelming mix of "But what isn't important?"

Luckily, there is something called a prairie vision, a prairie view, indeed, the prairie contrast: peaceful nothingness that can help bring things back into focus. No matter what the season is, in this place where the heart resides there is some aspect of nature and the outdoors capable of pulling you away from your daily routine and worries while offering a broader, more self-fulfilling, perspective, one that puts you back in the driver's seat.

Some things you might decide to do—gaze out on a golden-tipped wheat field before harvest; let a fishing guide take you out on the Missouri River on a clear day when the water's sparkly surface emits streams of magical, sunlit rays; soak up the sun on a warm autumn day when the sunflowers droop in abundance; go sledding down a gently yielding prairie hill; find a pond with a thick cover of ice for skating; walk through the prairie on a lovely spring day in search of wildflowers. Anything offering a reprieve from the hectic pace, the mundane, the millions of things you *must* do, the narrowing of vision that seems to occur in our daily lives as we repeat schedules and tasks and conversations. The prairie scene, in contrast, will fill your imagination with pleasing, multidimensional images; it will speak directly to your soul. I am reminded of summer evenings, prairie evenings, when the outside world feels distant, almost nonexistent. Picture this in your mind's eye.

The sun is setting ever so slowly—the sky, artistic stretches of amber and peach—and the air is warm, at least eighty degrees; a slight June breeze enters from the east as cattle and horses graze in a nearby pasture, as meadowlarks chime in, their melodic call familiar, comforting. And surrounded by greenish-brown prairie grass swaying back and forth in rhythmical fashion, we walk toward the setting sun. The ground is dry, causing a crinkling noise as we walk, disturbing the blanket of silence. Much like mounds of fall leaves, the grasses silently welcome, offering beauty, natural strength, composure, and certainty. Surely by now, competing thoughts that cry out for attention like a long row of spoiled children have grown silent. And the "do it faster, do it better, do it now" voices that reverberate through your psyche may have likewise given up, grown calm and quiet.

With the prairie's aura wrapped around you, it is almost a certainty that your thoughts have stopped swirling around like overworked honeybees: Now you are the wise and knowing captain of your ship. A bit like coming home to yourself, it is a place you once knew but quietly abandoned long ago in the maddening rush to get where you have to go next.

Where the Heart Resides

Yet believe it or not, taking time for ourselves is one of those important things often neglected in today's world; and yes, it may take the sweet, innocent melody of a prairie meadowlark to remind us of this.

MAKING THE CONNECTION

As a young person quite eager to explore the world beyond my immediate surroundings, I mistakenly concluded that the prairie's pull was something to resist, or ignore, as I simply could not understand why the immense lands, the windswept terrain without bright lights, apparent action, or excitement insisted on being such a strong force in my life. And I wondered why the area had such a grip on my heart when it seemed time to be free of all that, to move on to other things—more visible, outward signs of life—that simply had to be more interesting. But, like other things I have known, the more I resisted the prairie's compelling spirit, the more I questioned its subtle teachings and truths, the more its very essence echoed through my mind like the wise words of a grandparent or a dear friend, refusing to be silenced. But in my surrender, I found peace and happiness. Unexpected, unexplained, yet true, as true as true can be.

With this liberating revelation, I realized two things: The time spent growing up in the middle of nowhere was an experience to be treasured, not overlooked or diminished by myself or those who lacked appreciation for the place. Like Thoreau's famous journey into the woods, the prairie can be a wonderful place to "live deliberately, to front only the essential facts of life."

But I also came to realize that while the lands offering so much incredible beauty were not my enemy, neither were they as somber, silent, or passive as once perceived, seemingly uninvolved and unrelated to the "outside" world: In many ways, this land was the world, everything else just an artifact designed to support the nuances and demands of contemporary society.

When I finally made the connection, seemingly obvious, yet another prairie truth fell into place: It wasn't corny and unsophisticated to care deeply about an isolated land with few people and so little "place" in a modern, fast-paced world. And even though visitors looking for man-made marvels that glitter and glow in the dark were easily turned off or intimidated or downright perplexed by the area (the wide-open spaces make plenty of outsiders feel jittery and confused), I knew the power of the land, I understood its value to humankind, and eventually I came to terms with my prairie heart—its dictates, its wisdom, and, most of all, its trusted place in my life.

It became clear to me that our lives should be filled with "heart," so if your heart has moved on, grown quiet or overly somber, surely it is time to chart a new course. To settle for less implies several things: First of all, it will be difficult to even identify the important things if your life has slipped into a dark, unhappy state; second, a life without heart is a disservice to society, holding others back, keeping people from seeing the deeper, more meaningful truths life is meant to reveal; and third, when there is a lack of heart, there is a lack of honesty (something is not quite right, and usually we know it), and within this context, we cheat and belittle ourselves, blaming everything, everyone around us for a miserable, unhappy existence—one that is, at a minimum, out of sync with the cosmos.

But then again, prairie life encourages an honest approach to life: Unadorned and unencumbered, the land itself looks "honest," its soul clearly visible to all who wish to see it. Clearly, the prairie lands encourage us to assess, openly and honestly, what is truly important, and what is not. As a symbol of life's natural simplicity—complete, pure, lofty yet down to earth—the land imparts a back-to-the-basics theme with the dignity and precision of a spiritual advisor, one who is most trusted, one who knows the heart of every man, woman, and child regardless of race, religion, or family heritage; one who dares to speak the truth in the face of rejection, ridicule, and unkind hilarity.

This is the prairie's gift to us at the turn of the century and beyond; not a useless, bleak land, as many conclude prematurely, without thought, understanding, or exploration, rather, the boundless space, all that it contains and symbolizes, is a prized possession without a price. Not to be owned or locked away, prairie land, gracious and charming just as it is, is to be celebrated for all it represents, for all it has come to mean to so many. For the many tears it has evoked from people over the years, for the sheer joy, the love, and the wonder the prairie inspires in those who gaze upon it with a smile of compassion, appreciation, and hope.

All of us appreciate the Dakota skies which, clothed in sparkling stars
by night and bathed in the light of a glorious sun by day,
sustain our bond with nature and lift our view and thoughts to
other things than the world's tears.

—ROBERT ADAMS,
"DAKOTA SKIES,"
South Dakota Magazine

✌

RAISE SOME CHICKENS

Why does a successful rancher who can afford to go to the local grocery store and buy as many chickens—frozen or fresh, chopped or whole— as he wants or needs, buy a crate of chicks? Yellow, fluffy, chirping, busily pecking around for seeds or bugs, oblivious to the charming little girl standing next to the wooden crate with a big smile on her face.

Why do people take pets—cats, dogs, birds—into their homes in record numbers each year? And why do people all around the globe devote uncountable hours as volunteers for worthwhile projects? What about the time we give to family members, to friends and hobbies, to neighbors and community events? No real mystery, is it?

Helping other people, things, or interests along is a global pastime, raising chicks just one small example, a prairie example. But consider for a moment how wonderful the experience for a young child, boy or girl. Not because chickens are the most enchanting animals in the world nec-essarily, but more because she will cherish the positive memories well beyond her childhood; he will learn firsthand the wonder of growth and development; she will experience the demands and responsibilities of caring for a helpless creature dependent on the outside world for its survival. Prairie truths, that's all. Simple, basic facts that sometimes get lost in the everyday shuffle.

That, too, is a basic wonder of the prairie: The good things, tested, tried, and true, that we know about life, the basic, simple things that we know work, become more obvious and apparent in a setting allowing for greater visibility of the finer details—the connecting points in life that allow us a true glimpse into our humanity, our better selves.

Patterns, often habits of unknown origin, when taken for granted or missed entirely in other settings stand out with a certain brilliance on the prairie. Even the small things like taking a step back to see the importance and value derived from letting a young child raise some fluffy, yellow chicks.

Like the opening chapter quote from an article called "Dakota Skies" suggests, simple things like brilliant stars in the distance, in the blackened prairie sky, that appear each night remind us of the good things, the happy things, in life. The things and people that, when nurtured along, when cared for, have the power to reward us in so many intangible, often surprising, ways.

Do you set the stage, consciously or unconsciously, for this kind of surprise in your life, allowing for the magical, the miraculous? Do you open your heart and mind to the simple goodness of sharing yourself with others—more or less fortunate or on an equal plane? It makes no difference in the end; what does make the difference is this: You showed the heart and the good sense to seize the moment, to view an opening as an opportunity to give of yourself in a meaningful way. The size and magnitude of the project or person is clearly not the issue; the process—the involvement, time, energy, and loving attention—that goes into something or someone is what counts. Just being there for another person might be all it takes, or caring about someone who no one seems to view in a positive light. Maybe it is a matter of giving someone a second chance. A first chance perhaps.

One prairie resident put it this way: "When you give of yourself it takes the focus off yourself . . . by doing this, the problems we face seem not so great." One man who lives close to the land mentions the satisfaction he gets from offering fatherly advice every now and then, how much he enjoys helping people better their lives; he talks about loaning money to a friend when he didn't have the funds to spare. And our pioneer lady, Frances Jones, believes "it is easier to give than to receive." Even when she was going through a tough time herself, when it might have been easier to have turned away, Frances felt she gained "peace of mind" from continuing to give of herself. She also shares a story about a man who once rented a room from her but was unable to pay the rent, and how later on, he mailed her five dollars in every letter, eventually over-paying her. "I was more than paid," she explains.

So when life seems dull and lackluster, even when it seems par-ticularly spectacular, there is something to be said, something simple yet powerful, for the healing, healthy ways of the heart. In a society, indeed a world, that serves up a strong dose of ill will each day, the prairie way reminds us of the need to "do good." As a carryover from the pioneer days, perhaps, or maybe the land itself, in representing a strong yet subtle force in the lives of those who experience its sphere of influence on a daily basis, there remains a noticeable feeling of vulnerability on the prairie. Endearing, really. Maybe even a bit charming, for the net effect creates a need among many residents to openly acknowledge the plight of every living person and creature to survive, to prosper, to make the best from the worst. And from this recognition springs a natural desire to help others along, because in a place where cattle, horses, wind, im-mense wheat fields, prairie grass, and a heavenly sky still predominate, no one dares to take on the elements alone.

Like courting disaster, an overly confident ego does not last long on the prairie; someone or something is always prepared to trim it down to size. For you see, the prairie and its people are realists at heart, contending with excess or false personal pride by gently reminding themselves and each other that hard times are just over the next hill.

While it may or may not be true in the literal sense, life has a way of tossing out a mixed bag: no matter who you are, no matter where you live, no matter what you do. And while this is not meant to imply that we should wallow in our own misery, welcoming misfortune as if it were a best friend, something we deserve, or worse yet, a reflection of an unlucky soul, a certain amount of peace and positive, life-enhancing energy is released when we accept the ways of the world by giving back to the Universe.

A PRAIRIE DICTUM

In a society that prides itself on "getting ahead," and definitely at this point in our nation's history, it is beneficial to consider the spiritual and emotional healing that is made possible by practicing this simple prairie dictum: Personal power, personal gain can best be augmented by honoring the cyclical nature of the cosmos. As if the world somehow seeks balance, harmony, and, curiously enough, stability within movement, there is wisdom and honor in acknowledging the unseen forces governing our existence.

FROM THE INSIDE OUT

When you unwrap a gift, what is at the heart of the package—something light and friendly, or an intimate, deeply felt gesture, or something delightfully unique? With rare exception, the true message, the point of the gift, reveals itself best on the inside. The wrapping, a gift's exterior, merely a cover, an attractive piece of paper suggesting a birthday, anniversary, holiday, or other special occasion. Even with an outrageous bow or colorful curls of ribbon, it is the inside component that counts. And so it is when we give of ourselves.

Our thoughts, intentions, concern and caring, perceptions, courage, and honesty—it all comes from the inside. Words, for instance, when used to communicate ideas, feelings, beliefs, or encouragement possess amazing power; words can provide incredible gifts without measure or price. By providing a perfect vehicle for what is on the inside, words, when written or spoken, sometimes unspoken, provide priceless commodities: freedom, dignity, choice, love, passion, or the wonderful empathy of genuine friendship. Often, words communicate new ideas or compassion, maybe an insight that has been a long time in coming. Or a secret worry, a doubt that seems overwhelming when held inside, isolated from the world. Fears, real or imagined, sorrow and sadness, frustration or confusion. *Anything and everything.*

Yet how often do we overlook the power of words to shape our daily existence, to guide our children, to lessen our fears? Instead, when giving to others, we too often turn, sometimes automatically, to the external world; we give others the "wrapping" without the contents. We send expensive cards with nothing more than a signature, without a handwritten note that comes from the inside, from the heart; we buy something we like, something with no real meaning for the recipient; we throw a party out of a sense of duty or obligation, to impress the neighbors perhaps, when mere words that convey true understanding, concern, and appreciation might have meant so much more.

While there is a time and a place for these things, in our haste to keep up, stay in, follow the maddening crowd, fit in or adhere to the latest fad, we succumb to external pressures and visions that, when used indiscriminately, do not help us build bridges to each other; rather, they destroy them. As a people, for many, many reasons, we simply have not accepted the limited role of artificial constructs, external aids, that are incapable of providing lasting warmth, meaningful connection, respect, and love.

When was the last time you paid someone a compliment—one you meant, one that required perception and awareness of the individual on an internal level, one he or she remembered, maybe even shared with someone else?

I am reminded of a popular movie, *As Good as It Gets,* and of the scene where Carol (Helen Hunt) asks Melvin (Jack Nicholson) to pay her a compliment—right now, or she's gone. As is fitting to the role, he hems and haws, looks skyward, rolls his eyes, and so on as he tries to come up with an acceptable response. Finally, in truly surprising fashion, Melvin says that she makes him try to be a "better man." And later on in the movie, toward the end, when he is still trying to convince her that he is for real, not just some eccentric author looking for a vulnerable catch to boost his shaky ego, he shares his true impressions of her, explaining how he is able to see below the surface to what is special and wonderful about her . . . on the inside. Of course, she melts, and the movie winds down to its expected happy ending at the neighborhood bakery at four in the morning, before dawn has immersed the city streets in activity, in the external world.

A wonderful example of the incredible power of words, of being able to see the truth, the innate goodness and humanity within another person, this really is as "good as it gets." And in terms of forging a heartfelt bond of long-term duration between two people, very little seems to compare with the couple's ability to see and appreciate the essence, what is on the inside, at the center, the core, of each other—the part most people overlook, fail to understand, or misconstrue. Prairie life sets a good example for this.

By persistently encouraging us to look beneath the obvious for what is real, we are reminded of the need to give others something of true value; we are reminded to give of ourselves.

A CHILDHOOD DIARY

As a young person, I, like most people, recorded my private thoughts in a diary or journal, usually promptly discarded as thoughts of *Who might find this?* always won out against thoughts of *Gee, it would be fun to look back and read this someday*. And the other day when my mother told me how she had happened across her Girl Scout diary, one from her elementary school years, I thought about this again. Amazed to find that it still existed, she enjoyed the memories her discovery provided. It occurs to me that if others noticed the things about us we wish they would see or come to understand, childhood diaries would not have to be such a secret, such a worry, such a risk.

We have created a society of strangers in many respects, and only history will inform us of the net effect, I'm afraid. But if everyone were to share more of their internal world, maybe we would find there is little to fear but fear itself, as someone once said. Maybe we would find our way back to our hearts, our only true salvation perhaps.

Naturally, I am not advocating the careless, indiscriminate, or insensitive sharing of personal feelings or thoughts, rather, just enough to keep us "real" in the eyes of others. We live in a world of some danger, hidden or manifest, so our safety, the well-being of others, is of critical importance. Yet if we succumb to our fears without a fight, or go overboard in creating layers and layers of self-protection, perhaps we are merely supporting the forces that would destroy our very humanity—something glorious and fine and most worthy of our protection.

The movie *Patch Adams* comes to mind. Starring Robin Williams and based on a true story, he plays a medical student who is committed to change: Patch makes it his personal crusade to improve the quality of life for patients and puts up a valiant effort to alter the "system." In the movie, he confronts a lot of fear, and, of course, meets with considerable resistance; but he does prevail, to a point. He is an inspiration, revealing what we are all capable of in our finer moments.

Basically, he is fighting for people—medical patients—to be treated with basic regard and dignity; that their internal needs also be accounted for in an environment dedicated to their "healing." It makes tremendous sense, and is symptomatic of broader issues in our society. As we move farther and farther away from the "human element," due to the serious issues that plague our civilization at the dawn of the twenty-first century, we further jeopardize our future with each waking breath.

It is indeed an appropriate time to glance back at the pioneers of the prairie, at the men and women who shaped this country, to ask ourselves, *where in the world are we going*? Are we losing our capacity to care, or is there simply too much to care about? What can we do to change things before it is too late? Look inside your heart for the answers; share your truth.

I learned a prairie secret:
take the numbing distance in small doses
and gorge on the little details that beckon.

—WILLIAM LEAST HEAT-MOON,
PrairyErth

⸎

USE A ZOOM LENS

This book would not be complete without consideration of the seemingly insignificant details in life—inconspicuous, layered, or laced throughout—that can easily be overlooked in the daily shuffle: the whirlwind pace, the fast lane, the spellbinding dance of life that engrosses and absorbs us, mesmerizing our minds until we sometimes lack the ability or the will to *see* the important details.

Of course, on a basically flat land with nothing but rolling prairie for backdrop, where people and trees are treasured commodities, where nature calls the shots, "little things" are not so very little—a matter of context, I suppose. But also revealing because of the enhanced focus, the balanced perspective, which is silently nurtured along among the people. You see, these are not people who have already "seen it all," not according to society's definition anyway; and clearly, not according to what is "in" and what is "out."

What they have seen, however, is *this*: the amazing survival of livestock, gardens, crops, and fledgling trees when things looked dismal and hopeless; relentless snows, punishing winds, and parched earth, dry and rock hard but somehow renewable each spring; pinkish morning skies that tease the imagination, stretching overhead with the promise of something other than intense, blistering heat. People of the prairie, those who take active note of their prairie surroundings, in particular, have witnessed a lot of life at its most fundamental, sometimes less than glorious, sometimes marvelous and miraculous level. And from this rather lofty perch, many have willingly relinquished the need to submit to society's standards, of what it supposedly means to "live."

Instead, many have yielded to the powers that be, and in taking the prairie into their hearts and lives, their vision is restored; they are empowered to "see" life from a position of strength, quiet, and calm. Not a mad dash to follow the crowd, a circus act intended to elicit cheers, laughter, and applause, the prairie culture is more apt to reward and nurture an attitude of appreciation for the priceless details inherent in the milieu all mortals share. Life-sustaining details that when seen with clarity and precision, when looked at close up, as if through a camera's zoom lens, can renew a belief in the ultimate value of everyday life, of its obvious beauty: a new calf or colt, an apple tree blanketed in white blossoms in the spring, a proud robin eager to display its squirming catch after a morning rain shower, a field of sunflowers, beaming faces turned toward a brilliant sun.

Maybe just a tiny bow in a child's hair, the hesitant notes of a first piano recital, or the unexpected smile of an elderly man in a wheelchair; sometimes it is nothing more than the quiet lisp of moving water, a light breeze running through trees, camouflaged deer or pheasant, bare tree branches thick with winter frost, a lilac bush in full bloom. A prairie list, part of an endless list, would include all of the above and more.

Yet how often do we forget, or fail, to look, to *see* the mighty details of life so capable of enlarging our sense of self and well-being? We rush by and over them to accomplish the "important" things; yet I have to wonder if we are not missing the picture entirely. When life gets out of focus there is a common tendency to turn, or run, away, to slight, even disconnect from priorities, people, and established purposes that are at the core of our existence until something happens to bring us back to our senses, until something occurs to bring things back into their proper view. Ideally, from my perspective the proper view is a prairie view, where the "incidental" side of life, the part often discounted by those who have lost sight of the value of life's most sacred, awe-inspiring moments, is not brushed away or simply tucked in around the edges in haphazard fashion. Where common moments that somehow embody the true spirit of life generate a warm smile, a pat on the back, a wink reflecting shared understanding and appreciation.

For the prairie view, you see, is of the soul-wise variety—not from purposeful design necessarily and not because of modern-era books instructing prairie dwellers on how to put more "soul" into their lives; rather, the soul-wise ways of the people reflect a way of life, a humble, unpretentious way that has been around a long time. Sustained and finely honed by the elements, by the simple economies of a rural environment in the middle of nowhere, by a vast terrain that is loved by many as though it were a member of their family, the prairie's soul has had its rightful say:

In gazing out upon me look not for Bright Lights; look not for the magnificence of the Golden Gate Bridge, the power of the Statue of Liberty, imposing mountaintops or masterful ocean tides; but gaze out upon me for comfort and inspiration against the harshness of the world. And in so doing know that the lessons of this land are many, its triumphs seemingly few, its sorrows often unbearable. Yet the wildflowers of the prairie still bloom each spring as gentle breezes still whistle through the prairie grass with a melodic, peaceful sound, as all sorts of wildlife still rustle around looking for a safe haven, as time marches on into the next century. As the morning dawns and the soul is once again awakened to another day, another love, another time.

With Mother, bread baking was an art, and mother would bake 8–12
loaves twice a week. She used her own live yeast, a sponge of yeast,
potato water, shortening, salt, flour . . . mixing and
letting it rise at night.

—LORNA BUNTROCK HERSETH,
Autobiography

✑

SPICE IT UP

From the basic standbys that most of us depend on to elaborate affairs featuring the finest menus, food preparation and consumption play central roles in our lives: physical survival, a sense of purpose and a predictable routine, companionship with friends and family, a pleasant backdrop for social events, and, for some, a creative outlet.

This sometimes mundane aspect of life can also offer us an avenue for emotional self-expression and caring, for linking hearts and minds in a shared need to define our lives with concern for others. Imagine the countless number of relationships forged over food: simple, extravagant, mildly interesting to plain boring; it doesn't seem to matter.

As a primary building block dating back to the inception of life as we know it, nurturing ourselves and those around us with a variety of food comes naturally. Like emotional, spiritual, and intellectual sustenance, there is a positive connection between sharing culinary talents with others and a renewal of our physical energies. On the prairie, in the city, no matter where you happen to reside, this is a simple fact of life, one we recognize and accept without further thought. But at this point in history, it is worthwhile and interesting to consider the changes taking place around us: multitudes of fast-food chains, demanding schedules that encourage us to "drive through," prepackaged grocery items with a list of ingredients unknown to man or woman, rushed dinner hours turned into "dinner minutes," fewer *shared* meals with meaningful conversation and human interaction.

Granted, some of these societal "adjustments" can be linked to bigger, broader changes taking place around the world, and we all have to keep up . . . to a certain extent. Yet if we still hope to be masters of our own destiny, at least to a useful degree, then why not look at this matter from a soul-wise perspective? Why not peek into our hearts for guidance? There is merit in asking ourselves if we are comfortable with a "drive-through" selection, with lessened emphasis on preparing food from natural ingredients in a manner that is satisfying and pleasing to the heart and soul, with an "always in a hurry" atmosphere around the table, in front of the television, in the car, or standing in the kitchen.

Excess time is a luxury most of us don't have, so naturally there is a growing emphasis on "quick and easy," yet in moments of silent worry or frustration, do you ever feel like you inadvertently signed up for the wrong race, one you did not intend to participate in? Do you practically inhale your lunch, skip it entirely, or eat something you do not enjoy in the slightest—just to hurry through the process, to get lunch behind you and quickly move on to the next task? It happens; you are not alone.

But let's take a few minutes to peer into the prairie scene once again; perhaps there is a bit of wisdom lurking there if we look carefully at a lifestyle still "catching up" with the rest of the world. And in glancing back, in looking at a culture based on its very own set of "tried and true" values, maybe we will come across a few ideas guaranteed to have a place in your life, too. Because the time to look is *now*, before unwanted patterns become part of your daily routine.

A PRAIRIE COOK

What is a prairie cook, what does he or she look like, what role does cooking play in his or her daily life? Stepping back in time to the days of threshing crews, large families of ten or so children, and groups of cowboys who rode together as they worked this or that ranch, a prairie cook was just about anyone who would take the job!

Short or tall, young or old, man or woman, married or single—if you could fry an egg or make a cup of coffee, your future was secure. And if you could start a fire in the middle of the prairie—without causing a prairie fire—so much the better, as the facilities were often rudimentary, consisting of "must-have" items only. Blackened pots and pans, a handful of dented tin cups, a cast-iron skillet, maybe a couple of bowls and a ladle for soup.

Time marched on, of course, and before long the prairie was dotted with more people, and since men were often needed outside, cooking soon became a female specialty. Some took to the task as if the sun wouldn't shine without their hard work, but others caved in under the pressure, leaving the heavy cooking to those next in line: aunts, sisters, daughters, mothers, grandmothers. A few brothers and uncles, maybe a cousin or two, and quite likely a stranger, "just passing through," could win a spot in the kitchen, too, as the workload, for some prairie cooks, was indeed incredible.

After a time conditions improved, but the demand for good cooks, for food preparation in substantial quantities, prevailed. Cooking for large groups was a highly valued skill on the prairie well into recent times. In certain settings, it is still an ability worth acquiring. In spring, summer, and fall, large farming and ranching operations hire extra help, "hired hands," for harvesting or the branding of livestock, but nowadays, the ranch owner's wife gets the responsibility for feeding the "help," for providing large quantities of food morning, noon, and night. Of course, she is free to recruit additional help—if she can!

So, all in all, a prairie cook is any brave soul who has a talent for keeping things warm, a good sense of humor (most would rather laugh than cry), a willingness to serve a group of less than gracious or sophisticated people, usually men, who are hungry beyond belief, and a rare ability to work and cook with whatever is available, to improvise without complaining. I almost forgot—this individual must also be willing to work for so-so wages or room and board. Or, in the case of a lucky spouse who has become the resident prairie cook, for nothing more than a hurried smile, a quick "thanks" offered on the way out the door.

You are right, of course: The job, the role, is not particularly glamorous.

Yet from this not so enviable vantage point, prairie cooks have passed down, through the generations, impressions and qualities worth considering, even now, at the turn of the century. And even those who may not actually qualify as "prairie cooks," women and men who cook for small families perhaps, or just for themselves, with modern conveniences in a citylike atmosphere, have something to offer. For recipes circulate like dollar bills on the prairie, where there is still plenty of emphasis on homemade cooking and all the heartwarming things that go with it: colorful gardens, a mix of vegetables and flowers; canned, baked, and pickled goods; prairie potlucks; treasured family recipes and cooking traditions that have been passed down for generations.

Wileta Hawkins, mother to three sons and certainly a "pioneer" in her own right, has created two family cookbooks, but one of her favorite recipes is still her mother's cream pie.

Mix together 2 cups heavy cream, 1 cup sugar, ½ cup flour, and 2 teaspoons vanilla, then pour mixture into an unbaked pie shell and bake about 30 minutes at 350 degrees until golden brown.

PRAIRIE ART

While good cooking is a cherished form of prairie art, the opportunity to share talent, resources, affection, and companionship adds to its creative appeal and makes it central to the prairie lifestyle. If a neighbor is down on his or her luck, if there is cause to celebrate, if someone's garden has produced massive quantities of rhubarb, cucumbers, tomatoes, or corn, most will gladly see this as a chance to step into the kitchen. Not out of a sense of duty or obligation, but from a desire to nurture others in a way that comes naturally to most prairie dwellers: After all, there is something simple and unpretentious about it. It fits the area like a charm, a perfect prairie charm, one that sustains a belief in the everyday value of what is attainable and realistically satisfying. One that enhances daily life in a way that is reminiscent of bygone days when life on the prairie was a survival test in every sense of the word. (There are those who would argue that life on the prairie is *still* a test to survive, and depending on occupation, goals, or personal preferences, that may be the case.)

But in backyards, on farms of all sizes, there are also wonderful gardens that produce the most gorgeous fruits and vegetables. And the flowers that are often grown as garden borders add a special brilliance to the welcoming scene. As if planted with tremendous care, as if loved openly by those who enjoy the pleasing mix of summer colors—white, purple, orange, blue, and yellow—garden flowers add a special touch to nearly any setting. Nothing out of the ordinary typically; if you were to tour a few prairie gardens, you would find some marigolds, petunias, hollyhocks, iris, chrysanthemums, and tiger lilies. Maybe a few rose-bushes here and there, although they must be a hardy variety if they are to survive a prairie winter.

Tucked in many prairie yards are wild rosebushes with pink and yellow blooms, lilac bushes, and spirea bushes featuring dainty white clusters on slender stems. The wild rosebushes are my favorite, but please do not compare wild roses to long-stemmed roses that require more care-ful attention, for wild roses have a natural, spontaneous beauty that can-not be duplicated. Covered with thorns, however, pruning the wild rosebush can be a small challenge; and keep in mind as you clip a tiny bud for a bowl of roses that bees love these roses, too. Their fragrance is fresh, clear, and soft, perfumelike, captivating, and full of allure. But being "wild" roses, they can be difficult, if not impossible, to transplant. With a very long taproot, you will need to offer this rosebush plenty of quiet appreciation if you want it to adapt to new surroundings with any degree of success.

It is easy to see how the charm of the prairie is displayed in a purposeful sense through the natural beauty the people create in their bountiful gardens, how the prairie endears itself to us time and time again.

Good food, often traditional in origin, wonderful cooks who delight in working with their hands, hearts, and souls to create pleasing dishes for long-awaited guests, spur-of-the-moment company, and family mem-bers, along with a joyous spirit of adventure, are hallmarks of the prairie kitchen. One woman I interviewed for this book pointed out that birthday cakes were her specialty, while several mentioned the companionship and closeness that cooking has provided over the years.

Where the Heart Resides

And my mother, who we love to tease by calling her "Betty Crocker," can dance circles around any big city chef when it comes to creating culinary delights.

A few of her specialties include blueberry pancakes with a hint of cinnamon, caramel rolls that her grandchildren think are good enough to "die for," rhubarb-strawberry pie with a touch of lemon, and tonight, as I rummage through the many recipes passed down over the years, I see one for Aunt Sally's Beer Pancakes.

Stir together 2 cups biscuit mix, 2 tablespoons sugar, ½ teaspoon cinnamon, and a dash of nutmeg. Combine 5 beaten eggs with a ½ cup beer and 2 tablespoons vegetable oil. Then add egg mixture to dry ingredients, stirring just until moistened. Batter will be lumpy. Cook on hot, lightly greased griddle. Makes 10 to 12 (4 inch) pancakes.

I don't dare discuss her chocolate cake, which is not for the weak of heart, but her only secrets, she says, are to follow the directions (if you are a beginner) and put plenty of heart into the task at hand so others will sense the special attention—the time, thought, and skill—that went into the dish. And now, as I picture her in the family kitchen at all times of the day and busily focused on whatever she was preparing, apron pulled tight, hair pushed back from her face, which was sometimes red when she was really moving, I recall the countless hours devoted to cooking and I hope we did not take it for granted; although, I suppose, like the children of most families, we did.

She enjoyed it so much; "Time flies when I'm cooking," she would say, and it seemed so natural, so easy for her that I am quite confident we failed to remember that this was still "work." Her skill and assuredness in the kitchen, the obvious pleasure cooking gave her, made it way too easy for us to forget.

LEMON MERINGUE PIE

I grew up with three sisters and one brother; we all learned how to cook— a prairie necessity, in my mother's eyes—so none of us is a slouch in the kitchen. My brother, in fact, owns a food-manufacturing company in Arizona; he (and his company, one he started from scratch) is a success story and much admired. His southwest specialty produces "ass-kickin'" salsa, gourmet hot sauces "from hell," and award-winning habanero pepper products. But *none* of us has mastered lemon meringue pie, another one of my mother's specialties. A beautiful sight when prepared correctly, it does have a certain zesty appeal, I guess. But it is such a "touchy" pie, such a tricky recipe, that most people, including myself, are intimidated by it . . . completely.

Yet in my mother's eyes, I feel sure I will not have earned my "cooking stripes" until I learn how to make lemon meringue pie. For those of you who want to give it a try, here is her favorite recipe.

Microwave for 4 to 5 minutes 1½ cups sugar, ⅓ cup cornstarch, 1 ½ cups water. In small bowl beat 3 egg yolks, add some of the hot mixture to eggs, stir, then add remaining yolks to hot mixture and cook 2 more minutes. Add ¼ cup lemon juice, 1 tablespoon butter, and pour in baked crust. For the meringue you need the 3 egg whites, ¼ teaspoon cream of tartar, 5 to 6 tablespoons sugar, and a dash of vanilla. Beat the whites and tartar until frothy, adding the sugar slowly, until mixture is firm and shiny. Add vanilla and place meringue on pie filling. Brown in 350-degree oven for 15 minutes.

That's it! So simple, I'm told.

I will never share this with my mother, but I am not sure I like lemon meringue pie. Could that be part of my reluctance, part of my fear of tackling this yellow-and-white dessert, which is hardly a prairie basic? That I will have to ponder for a time.

In the meantime, I will stick with simple things like chili, lasagna, pizza, tacos, and *cherry* pie—now that I can make! And while I would be happy to share my recipe, mine is standard, not difficult at all; the tricky part is to avoid the cherry pits that are left in the canned filling now and then.

And although it took many, many tries, I have finally mastered pie crust, but it was only because I lived in South Dakota at the time that I felt inspired to learn. It seemed to be my prairie duty, or my pioneer spirit come to life, so my confidence was up, and at long last, I prevailed. Two tips worth sharing: *Add 2 tablespoons confectioner's sugar to the flour and salt mixture if you like a sweeter crust, or for a puffier crust, add ¼ teaspoon baking powder to the dry ingredients.*

Otherwise, good luck! The best thing to do to learn how to make great pie crust is to practice.

No one is dissatisfied,

not one is demented with the mania of owning things. . . .

—WALT WHITMAN,

"SONG OF MYSELF"

BORROW IT,
DON'T BUY IT

Self-sufficiency has its place, there is no doubt. Yet like any plus, this mode of operation can become a minus when taken to extremes. Absolute independence from those in our midst, even if truly possible, would insulate and contain us well beyond healthy dimensions. Needing other people, other proclivities and opinions, and sources of emotional and intellectual support, as long as not overdone, requires us to reach out to others; it keeps us humble and connected to forces outside ourselves.

We all seem to realize that relationships of all shapes, sizes, origins, and destinations provide emotional fuel for our earthly journey: by giving us an opportunity to return the gift of caring and concern; by nurturing us through the storms of life; by helping us pilot our way across nebulous skies. Without human interaction, the gentle, abiding flow of wants, wishes, and worries comprising the silky web of life—its precarious stretch, its invisible dangle and sway from limb to limb—there would be a certain collapse of all we hold dear; our days on earth would float away in meaningless bits and pieces like amorphous pieces of cotton drifting free from cottonwood trees in the summer. Without a doubt, what a sad state of affairs it would be, for built into our psyches is the very natural, very human need to experience ourselves in relation to others, to discover our own unique truths through the people we encounter during a lifetime. We test our strengths, uncover our weaknesses, dismiss or overcome our limitations, celebrate our accomplishments, recover from our misconceptions, all within the context of *we*.

So why do we stumble around in the dark trying to go it alone when a joint effort, the group or team approach, could smooth and show the way? And, as is the stated focus of this chapter, why do we insist on buying everything instead of sharing resources more readily with those around us? Have we forgotten the lessons of old, prairie lessons about the value of lending a helping hand, of loaning or giving something away without strings, expectations, or strong feelings of ownership?

Are we too attached to the "things" we own, the ideas we have, the skills we possess, the wisdom we have picked up along the way, maybe even our love and concern for those around us, for humanity? Do we hold on to these things, these parts of ourselves, waiting for just the right time, just the right moment, to share them?

Or, worse yet, do we fail to share our feelings, thoughts, skills, or ideas, even on the most cursory of levels? This may read like twenty questions, but there is really one question at the heart of the matter: As a civilization, are we overly competitive, to the point of being destructive?

Everyone seems to thrive on competition these days—beating out the next guy, getting there first, showing someone up—yet this path seems to be taking us farther away from our finer, nobler, human qualities, and to me, these are admirable attributes worth preserving. Like the prairie lands, however, if we fail to place a value on life-enhancing, life-preserving ways of being, disintegration and eventual extinction may follow. When this nation was young, when the settlers moved west filled with hopes and dreams (and yes, fears), they seemed to cling to a strong belief in themselves, but many knew the value of interdependence, of being able to rely on others with material or emotional support when the need arose. Survival, of paramount concern, encouraged and required faith in others, but the prairie mind-set, in a general sense, seemed to be one of realistic regard for life's unpredictable turns, and thus the eventual need to reach out for assistance.

In short, borrowing necessary items or products was okay, simply confirming the ways of the world, the natural law of averages. In sensing the shared nature of their precarious journey, neighbors helped each other out, valuing the need to be needed, of being able to reciprocate when the time came. And sometimes I think they gathered strength from this recognition, from their own form of self-sufficiency. By banding together, by helping people out in a spirit of survival, there was less emphasis on competition, less dependency on "store-bought" items (assuming they could find a store in the first place), but since that era, things have changed.

Now people rush to the store almost automatically, wanting to pick out what is new, novel, or expensive: to impress a neighbor or a friend, to stay on top of the latest fashions (trendy items do sell), to merely have something to do with their day, to buy what they need. The act of purchasing seems to have taken on a life of its own, and by giving some people a false sense of independence, the cycle is self-perpetuating.

It has been my observation, however, that a better balance could be achieved between borrowing and buying. This is *not* to recommend making a nuisance of yourself, but in an effort to keep energy flowing, to keep relationships vital, there is merit in reducing the number of "things" you absolutely must own. And in lightening your load, the items you dust and move around from this room to that, a simpler lifestyle may present itself as an unexpected reward, an added benefit. You may even feel more relaxed and comfortable, as if sailing away from a place you never liked in the first place, free at last.

SETTING THE RIGHT TONE

By controlling our need to buy everything, to own everything, we become more pioneerlike, and maybe, at this stage of our development, that is a blessing, a highly desirable outcome. By returning to forgotten times and ways, gingerly picking up the threads that made sense (and still do), a ray of hope can be generated—one that focuses the picture anew; one that signals us in new directions, cleverly reminding us once again that less is more.

One prairie resident, when asked about this topic, pointed out that "people are always borrowing . . . a pair of jumper cables for a dead battery, a pair of shoes. It's just something you do. You lend things when someone needs something, borrow if you need to." And a related comment came from a local rancher. "When I first started on this ranch in 1954, I had only one horse and had to borrow the neighbor's horse to round up cattle. Not really resourceful," he adds, "just didn't have the money to buy another one."

Either way, borrowing, because it seems convenient, friendly, and fun, or borrowing out of necessity, can keep our need for material possessions in line with the other, more important, things in life. So, regardless of where you reside, try to develop close friendships that allow for a healthy give-and-take. The mutual respect, the warm feelings of cooperation that develop, will ensure a happier tomorrow for us all.

I guess the interesting things that happen make life worth living.

Some are unhappy, but we can't pick and choose.

— FRANCES NICKEL JONES,

SOUTH DAKOTA RESIDENT, 1895

SEEK CHALLENGE, NOT COMFORT

Have you ever known someone who strikes you as living in a superficial realm? She seems out of touch with the complexities of life, continually looking for ways to ease her way through the day instead of taking on meaningful challenges; he seems happy skimming along the surface of life, too, never daring to commit to difficult, yet inspiring, goals, perfectly content to while away his time on earth seeking out fun and pleasure to the exclusion of real opportunities for personal growth and development, situations that ultimately force us to stretch beyond our comfort zones.

And strangely enough, even when life deals such individuals a series of losing cards, they somehow laugh it all off, stubbornly refusing to accept any turn of events that does not match their world view, their "happy-go-lucky" existence. In most instances, however, a catalyst appears on the horizon, one that mandates a significant amount of change, and to a degree at least, those who shun the more demanding side of life are eventually presented with a set of circumstances, often difficult and trying, that must be addressed. And only after trying to wiggle away do they succumb to the inevitable, digging deep within to uncharted territory—marvelous inner resources previously dormant and untapped.

Like a lightbulb starting to flicker, showing signs of life at last, these events are "wake-up" calls, and the people most affected by them are nearly always pleasantly surprised by what they discover about themselves when the chips are down—things like courage, self-discipline, determination, compassion, new skills (careers or relationships), personal insight, and self-awareness. Best of all, the person experiencing an emotional or physical jolt that cannot be ignored, the person who finally confronts himself or herself under challenging conditions may discover the true texture of life: the depth and richness and purpose of our lived experience.

Trying times can represent door openers—to ourselves, to those around us, to a life that is compelling in its own right—and even though we may not want to pass through a particular door, one that has, in some respects, been identified and opened for us (too painful, too foreign and frightening, too dark and dismal), a sort of assurance and comfort can be derived by venturing onward, through the dreaded passageway. Often the anticipation is worse than the reality; not only that, but when rough waters are successfully navigated, intangible benefits, such as self-confidence, self-respect, and greater personal strength can be garnered from the experience.

To be employed (and enjoyed) in a variety of contexts that follow, such attributes carry enormous, life-altering potential, and as an outgrowth of character-building experiences are indeed worthy of our pursuit.

The moral of the story is simple; it is one we know *instinctively*, yet it is also one we tend to shy away from: We are the sum of our life experience, and in seeking meaningful challenge, like the pioneers of the late 1800s, we are given an opportunity to expand, to discover who and what we are, to test our limits and beliefs, to succeed when the odds are against us, to have tried when failure, perceived or actual, is our only reward, to come to know the true shape of our personal integrity, all so we may have an opportunity to come to understand what we are made of, on the inside. When our only significant goal in life is to try to exist in a state of continual comfort, if it were even possible, the world fluctuates around us like a mystical, maniacal maze, our internal compass forever frozen at "safe."

MISTAKES WORK

A challenge can be too difficult, too steep; we all have our limits and limitations, our hang-ups and our frailties, actual or perceived disabilities to consider and work around. For these we lament: *Oh, woe is me.* And sometimes we disavow these parts of ourselves: *Who, me?* Occasionally, we pinpoint specific dimensions of our being for an overhaul, a New Year's resolution type of approach: *From here on out, I will watch less television, consume less sugar, write more love letters, work more puzzles, fly more kites, exercise daily, expand my mind by reading more books, walk the dog each morning, call Uncle Floyd at least once a year . . . I'll even quit polluting the earth unnecessarily. And starting soon, I'll begin the project that has been on my mind, my mental to-do list, for months, the one that will be difficult to finish. I'll do more volunteer work, too, appreciate what the world has given me, share it with others who are less fortunate.*

With echolike dependability, these words, *our* words, zing through our minds like old friends looking for a place to land amidst the mental debris. Yet for some reason they never find a permanent place to stop, only a temporary, sometimes momentary, place to pause until we are sidetracked, distracted by all that goes on around us, within us, or in spite of us. Still, the process offers us something, even though we may question the end result: a chance to fail, to forget, to question and rethink an answer, *to make a mistake*. If there is one thing society seems to have a low tolerance level for, this is it. Not to be used at random or to excess as an excuse for everything under the sun, making a mistake is completely normal. Yet even "honest" mistakes seem to make many people genuinely nervous and annoyed.

Wonderful tools to help us learn more about our inner workings, a few mistakes now and then are nothing but beneficial. (Obviously, I am not focusing on the sort of mistake that results in tragedy or any extreme.) Without a misstep here and there, an unintentional slip, we will never know if the challenge is too difficult; we will not know how to modify our course of action or how to accomplish anything of real significance.

Like lights on an airport runway, mistakes help us identify the true path so that we can aim ourselves in the right direction. As life's "indicators," our acceptance of the need to make mistakes can propel us forward. Growth, in fact, depends on an ability and a willingness to reach out, to err, and to modify behaviors, styles, or beliefs, and then to reach out again, letting the cycle redefine us until, eventually, over time, we replace the raw material with elements of wisdom.

Consider the multitude of mistakes the pioneers made; think about their hard-earned badges of courage; try to visualize their daily struggle, the fears and problems that threatened to snuff out their dreams. Character-defining moments—plenty of them—were built into their daily routine, and while they clearly suffered at times because of their mistakes, there is every reason to believe in the magic, maybe even in the poetry, of the accomplishment or self-understanding that manifested itself as a result of something quite fundamental: trial and error. We are never totally above it, never totally beyond it, not until we are completely out of the game, our last breath taken.

So why not zero in on a challenging goal, make it yours, give it your all. Find out if the challenge is too difficult or just deceptively so— there *is* a difference.

Modern-day prairie dwellers, while not at the mercy of the vast outdoors, the untamed wilderness, to the same extent as those who traveled before them nonetheless live in a place that seeks them out. That is the distinct impression one gets in traversing the prairie land. There is something about the openness that exposes and illuminates, causing newcomers to feel vaguely uncomfortable. Slightly vulnerable. Curiously present. And within this level of visibility, within the prairie's radar screen, hiding places are few; it can feel as if there is nothing to shield you from the Universe itself, the prying "eyes" of the world.

So life, in all its many shades of gray, must be dealt with. Even death, even the forces of nature that are awesome in their magnitude, splendid in their magnificence, ask to be recognized by all, no exceptions granted.

This feeling, this phenomenon, sometimes reminds me of a silent challenge: *Can you survive . . . here? Can you learn to love this vast terrain with its unpredictable ways? Can you accept the isolation, the contact and confrontation with prairie rattlers, wildlife that seems to own the land? Can you convince others of my worth, protect this land from those who would destroy it? And can you grow in compassion, grace, and dignity?*

The folks in Chicago and Iowa seemed to have bad manners,

and the Dakota people didn't have any at all.

That is what I liked best about them.

—WALKER D. WYMAN,

Nothing but Prairie and Sky

∽

D E V E L O P
A G E N E R O U S S P I R I T

Because their manners are so neatly tucked into a generous, warm-hearted way of life, it is easy to see why Bruce Siberts, a prairie settler who left his Iowa home in 1890, at the age of twenty-two, to seek his fortune farther west, did not detect any definable "manners" in those around him. Back then, and the custom has perpetuated itself, the focus seemed to be on genuine interaction that endears no matter what the occasion. Not in an artificial, short-lived way, not in phony, textbook fashion, and clearly not in an effort to win the etiquette award for the year. And in a similar vein, prairie manners will not be of the "fancy" variety either.

Certainly, you may find a few distinctions based on class—this is true of nearly all cultures, anywhere in the world—yet there remains an underlying "sameness" to prairie interactions that manifest as surface "manners." The thread that joins the external realm with the internal state is the generosity of spirit that runs through the heart of those who reside on the prairie lands I grew up with. You see, these are people who love to share whatever good fortune comes their way; and even when times are not so very wonderful, when misfortune appears, many, if not most, do not stop giving. It is not in their nature, for the most part, nor would it be true to their character. And while these terms may sound synonymous, there is a subtle difference to be considered.

Perhaps a matter of degree only, a question of to-what-extent-exactly, but it occurs to me that while we are born with character, perfected or flawed, we can still make minor adjustments, here and there, in relation to our nature. The difference is important because it makes room for something critical to our existence, namely, hope.

I mention this here because, if there is one thing we need, as a people, a culture, a society, and a civilization, it is just that, hope. It is the spark of the world's future, the reason we get up each day, the absolute point of meaningful, worthwhile goals. Some degree of hope is at the root of nearly everything we do—if you stop and think about it.

Without hope, how can we *hope* to change, and without change, will we not repeat ourselves, our questionable, less-than-admirable actions forever more? In other words, there would be little point in discussing the generous spirit of prairie dwellers if this fine quality could not be emulated by others.

And so it is that the "invaluable" worth of a generous spirit comes to light. In choosing to support others, in giving of ourselves when it would be easier to walk away, in taking time to care about the world and the people who inhabit it, we acknowledge the need for hopeful ways. As many prairie dwellers learned long ago, due to the power of the prairie, and commensurate with the presence of nature and its mysterious force, without *hope* the day could quite possibly not be endured. So they gave themselves and each other the gift of hope. And in their generosity, they watched themselves grow, saw their dreams take root. With equal enthusiasm, they saw those they supported along the way break new ground, as well—succeed and survive when the gods threw them every curve ball imaginable.

So today, as an overall observation, this orientation continues, and while some see this trait as compensatory, something people who live on the prairie—the middle of nowhere—engage in because they are unsophisticated hayseeds, because they are lacking in the finer graces, because they are naive or unworldly, nothing could be more inaccurate. In giving to others, even when conventional wisdom dictates otherwise, prairie lore, in being true to itself, suggests an enlightened approach, one that springs from the heart and soul of its own accord.

One longtime resident shared her thoughts on the subject, indicating that time and time again, whenever she reaches out to someone, she is rewarded. In particular, she recounts a situation when she invited someone into her circle of friends, only to discover that this person was going through a difficult time and thereby benefited greatly from her offer of support and friendship. How easy it is to envision a different scenario had she been afraid to extend a friendly hello, had she been worried about appearing foolish, assuming, or needy. "It just goes to show" (a popular phrase in South Dakota) that the wisdom of the world, the popularized, untested variety anyway, is often a source of *un*wisdom on the prairie.

So it is fortunate that most people who live "up there" hang on to their beliefs like treasured charms on a charm bracelet, even when influences from the outside filter in, causing some to question their ways, values, and style—momentarily. And even when they know others are laughing, making fun of them because they seem old-fashioned or silly or corny or any of the other clichés that circulate in an effort to describe behavior that appears usually kind or "nice," no strings attached, many simply look the other way, a choice most are happy to make. Living up to their personal standards and expectations is more important to them than appearing sophisticated or refined.

Not about to trade them in for popular approval, brownie points, or anything smacking of a sellout, it would take a leveraged buyout to get a majority of these people to adopt a new set of values that did not include a generosity of spirit. All year round, too, not just during holiday seasons!

But that can be fun to consider, too. As these lines from a poem by Karen H. Wee, as found in *The Book of Hearts*, suggest, Christmas celebrations on the prairie often resulted in crowded conditions that no one seemed to mind, or even notice. Just part of sharing whatever was available, big or small, a lot or a little.

> *O Tannenbaum, O Tannenbaum*
> *we sang each Christmas Eve*
> *at Grandma's house, Columbia, South Dakota*
> *in the late thirties, early forties, the fifties*
> *We stuffed fifty-three grandkids*
> *moms and dads, aunts and uncles*
> *into three skinny rooms.*

MORE THAN SURFACE MANNERS

Maybe it is a matter of attitude; maybe it is a question of what is really *real*; or then again, maybe it all comes down to doing what feels right, what makes us more, not less. I can only imagine how dreadful a society would be that is reduced to every-man-for-himself-type thinking. Yet are we not moving toward that sort of arrangement in a good number of urban settings? Places where the clamor to survive grows increasingly intense each day despite all the gloss and glitter, and despite the amazing reservoir of human potential that resides in our cities, along with the would-be cities, of the world.

Oddly enough, it looks as if we may have forgotten to consider the possible consequences: a world based on elitism, where only the perfect can survive; a world with no capacity for spiritual rejuvenation; a world absent of meaningful emotion and hope for the future; a world without concern for unknown forces that would willingly shield us from our hubris, our incredible blind spots; a world where we have truly lost our way—all in pursuit of a hollow victory, a feeling of smugness built on a shaky foundation.

Surely, if we were to listen to our hearts with a new willingness born of love for those around us, indeed, for ourselves and future generations, we would want to take stock of our surroundings from a reference point that offers us a chance of becoming more, not less. And once again, like newborns, we would display a capacity to evaluate what does and does not work. Not surprisingly, we might unravel the puzzle of the millennium: how to achieve true progress as a people without losing sight of our humanity.

It is my guess that it will take much more than surface manners to accomplish this twenty-first-century feat. Things like blood, sweat, and tears come to mind, along with the capacity to empathize with the struggles of those around us, to show an ability to making a commitment to rediscovering the power of heart in our daily lives. As a book called *Emotional Intelligence* by Daniel Goleman implies with its intriguing title, we cannot be truly "smart" without the active involvement of our emotional capacities. And at the risk of sounding sappy or provincial, nor can we be fully human. A "brilliant" person without a good heart, without good instincts for life, can be very dull indeed.

TRUE BLUE

A generous spirit can be born from a desire to remain loyal, genuine, and true hearted. "True blue," as people used to say in the forties and fifties. Or it can spring from a wish, a desire to give others the benefit of the doubt whenever possible, to try and understand or accept people just as they are or as they are trying to become. Generosity of spirit can also show itself when we acknowledge the shining moments of others: the true glitter of life when the soul sparkles, emitting a marvelous hue. Being genuinely happy for others when important events crystallize for them is a gift of heart like no other.

To be able to freely share in someone else's joy is a soul-enhancing attribute, one that accents the positive, providing confirmation in the ultimate worth of our journey. Happy news (or happy times) is always so much *happier* when there is someone to share it with; ideally, a person who appreciates the personal reasons that make the joyful occasion meaningful. Envy, jealousy, and mistrust too often spoil the moment, even between couples who share a committed, long-term relationship.

Possessing a generous spirit also allows you to overlook the insignificant slights that are an inevitable part of daily life. Usually on an unintentional basis, but we with some frequency, manage to hurt the feelings of those we come in contact with. Sometimes we realize what has occurred, but at other times we do not make the connection—unless it is pointed out to us. The ability to apologize helps; and when on the receiving end, it also helps to let the little things go by seemingly unnoticed. While keeping score is an alternative, people with ties to the prairie might be inclined to "just let it go." Not always, but in a setting that values constancy, friendship, and peaceful relations with others, maintaining close ties is a worthy goal.

LET IT LINGER

As we have learned, prairie residents are apt to loan money and other commodities even when they really do not have the extra to spare, and though you may think this unwise, imagine the goodwill they create and consider how this kind of generosity enhances relations with others.

The good feelings that are generated clearly lack a price tag, and in many respects, are a bonus that people can draw on indefinitely. And when this sort of healthy regard exists between people and nations, the world, as a whole, is indeed a better place; so when the opportunity arises to do something nice for someone, remember that the good feelings will linger on, well past the moment, well into the future, well beyond the generous act itself. A little bit like believing in Santa Claus, the key is to believe in the merit of giving gifts all year round.

Possessing a generous spirit shows that you, too, *believe*: in magic, in love, in acts of kindness big or small, in yourself, in all of mankind. In the universe and its capacity to support your many dreams, your travels, your private journey through a mystical land on a wonderful, make-believe ship called Life.

I was a scrawny, red-headed, freckle-faced tomboy as a young girl.

My mother used to express her love by saying,

"I love every freckle on your face."

— MARY JEWEL LEDBETTER,

SOUTH DAKOTA RESIDENT

❧

TELL STORIES

Preserving tradition, history, culture, even embarrassing moments reflecting the more intimate details of our lives offers solace against the unknown—the vastness of space, the inner reaches of the planet we call home, the mysteries of life and death, the amazing parts of ourselves, some good, some bad, that we will never come to know . . . no matter what. Confronted by a wide-open terrain, people who live on the prairie deal with the vast unknown on a daily basis, as the prairie itself bespeaks a time and a place that is neither here nor there. With an otherworldly presence, an aura of the infinite, the grass-covered lands remind us, on a purely visual dimension, of how much we don't know, can never know. Not *even* in a lifetime.

So, as an equalizer, as a means for coping with utter insignificance, recording thoughts, events, emotions, and special insights that keep us grounded while simultaneously passing information on to those who will follow is of vital importance. For this is the small part we have come to know: the tiny segment of life we have experienced, the gut-wrenching emotions we have lived through, the incredible joys we have known, the people who have crossed our path at the most surprising times, in the most unexpected ways—unforgettable points of connection (seemingly of the divine, certainly of the magical) when the world, for a brief time at least, makes sense, when we secretly rejoice in our good fortune at having met the one person whom we were so positive did not exist.

Maybe because the area's history is so readily apparent, prairie ways encourages the sharing of stories, formal or informal, embellished or factual, simple or complicated, that convey such moments—the ones we have somehow come to know. In contrast to the vast, uncharted domain, collectively the great unknown, such stories, no matter how detailed, naturally pale in comparison, yet at the same time offer us respite from an existence of meaningless uncertainty and vagueness.

GETTING IT DOWN

One way to "tell stories" is to record them in a journal or a diary, maybe in a book like this one, or maybe in a letter. Think of the wonderful ideas, the eye-opening revelations, oh, and the charming words of romance that have come to life, over the years, on paper. Since the beginning of recorded time, in fact, we have witnessed a seemingly innate need to detail our feelings and perceptions in a way and in a place where we can see the words, read them aloud, capture their true essence, indeed save and share them; in making the words "permanent," by getting them down on paper (or on any substitute), we feel more complete, as if we have somehow extended ourselves into the great unknown, and have effectively etched out a tiny spot in the universe that is concrete and purposeful and ours. Once recorded, sentiments are more real, more alive, and the part of life that seems to slip through our fingers, the part we cannot see or capture, is at least momentarily contained.

Is there anything more captivating than a poem that expresses exactly what you want to say? Anything more charming than a handwritten note that brings feelings to light in a way you thought impossible? What about the perfectly inscribed dedication, or the brief personal message attached to a gift of flowers, or the unexpected note of thanks? Length does not seem to be the issue. Rather, a few carefully chosen words can tell quite a story indeed! (Even those that might be better left untold.) The idea is to care enough to share, in writing, the thoughts and feelings that are too easily forgotten.

As noted in an article in *South Dakota Magazine* called "Pages of the Past," when you go back and read your own words—the ones you managed to get down on paper—you come to realize just how much has transpired along the way. This is according to a woman who has been recording her thoughts in diaries since 1931.

Gladys Schaffer, apparently very dedicated to recording the days of her life—no secrets, just "weather facts and homestead life"—seems to appreciate the grave importance of little things that when put down on paper take on a fresh quality, a dimension quite unlike the spoken word. *Lake Mitchell opened up for fishing. I didn't go as I had ironing to do. The folks went and they got their limit. Ten apiece.*

An invaluable look at the history of a people, personal journals provide a glimpse into the soul of the writer, into the collective spirit of a time and a place. Like stars on parade, the kind that travel through the spacious prairie sky so diligently and with such certainty, written entries, each one of them, each word, capture something so fleeting, an ephemeral moment of beauty and distinction that would otherwise be missed forever. For a life is generally not comprised of magnificence, glory, or notoriety; a life, most often, is built on the stupendous value of everyday activities that reflect the power of true understanding and connectivity with the universe, with other forces, seen and unseen. Because it is the things we do with frequency, some on a daily basis, that carve out our most precise image in the solar system, in the Milky Way galaxy, and needless to say, in our neighborhoods, workplaces, families, and personal relationships. Clearly, these taken for granted events, seemingly insignificant, are worth recording.

A SACRED TRADITION

The Native American heritage places a considerable amount of emphasis on verbal exchanges: in daily interactions, to record the passage of time, and to keep tradition alive. They believe the spoken word is a powerful means of communicating ideas, beliefs, a full array of possibilities— hopes, dreams, visions of the future—and ancient teachings; *talk* is at the heart of things.

This we have learned on the prairie from those who have shared the wise ways of the Native American legacy. In the anthology *Growing Up Native American*, edited and introduced by Patricia Riley, she writes: "The languages and oral traditions of Native American peoples have carried the thoughts and beliefs of their ancestors forward to their descendants in contemporary America. Passed from generation to generation through storytelling, oral traditions represent living libraries containing thousands of years of knowledge and history. . . ." And while she goes on to explain how turbulent times created the eradication of some native languages, Riley notes that "countless oral traditions still flourish and continue to evolve as new Native American storytellers add their voices to those of their ancestors. . . ."

In *I Tell You Now: Autobiographical Essays by Native American writers*, Simon Ortiz, a writer and a poet, states: "We come from an age-less, continuing oral tradition that informs us of our values, concepts, and notions as native people . . . despite the brutal efforts of cultural repression that was not long ago outright U.S. policy."

There is a certain vibrancy about the spoken word, a special quality that encompasses the totality of the individual who is talking or telling a story about the "good old days" (on the prairie, stories like this are alive and well), an inspirational story meant to uplift and motivate, or a childhood nightmare that mysteriously reoccurs later in life perhaps. When stories like these are shared aloud, a sacred sort of harmony can develop between the listener and the speaker. From intimate settings to formal gatherings involving hundreds of people, private conversations between couples, whispered tales or secret plans between brothers and sisters, all in all, the spoken word lends itself to intriguing themes, to poetic connections that sing with a certain purity of heart.

Fortunately, most prairie dwellers love to talk, so a good conversation is appreciated, and "talk" is often considered "entertainment" in its own right, no props needed. As a viable way to build bridges between young and old, men and women, poor and rich, races and religions telling stories on the prairie and elsewhere can do wonders for breaking through barriers, for developing rapport and understanding between diverse groups. Messages and teachings, otherwise resisted, when told in the form of a colorful or captivating story soften emotions and open doors to personal and spiritual growth. The most interesting thing about a good story is how its most meaningful aspects usually pertain to people of all walks of life. Stories with universal themes are able to supersede differences, perceived and real, by indirectly accentuating the commonalities—between nations, generations, religious and ethnic persuasions. And storytelling, by those who practice it on a pro-

Tell Stories   ∽ 181

fessional level or those who do it very informally, is an art form worth preserving.

By helping us keep in touch with our humanity, by nurturing our heartfelt connections to family and friends, to the people of the world as a whole, the oral tradition held in such esteem by most Native Americans is something to take note of. Because there is nothing like a good story to remind us, that, in the end, a life is the sum of mini-stories with a predefined climax and an ending that, while inevitable, is merely part of a frame around an entire life's story. By sharing our stories, we share ourselves, we give meaning to our lives.

GIFTS OF TIME

In her novel *Waterlily*, Ella Cara Deloria (a Dakota/Sioux born in 1889 on the Yankton Sioux Reservation in South Dakota), "tells the story of what life was like for a traditional Dakota woman from infancy to early adulthood." A passage from the book (originally published by the University of Nebraska Press), as included in the Riley anthology, clearly illustrates the sentiments, the poignant feelings of a young girl in relation to her mother and vice versa, that when carved out in words resemble treasured jewels:

To Waterlily these were memorable days, for this was the time she began to like her mother best and enjoy being with her more than with the other family members. Before, she had turned as readily to her grandmother, aunts, and other relatives as to her mother—it was the way of related families—but now she was learning to appreciate her mother for the rare and sympathetic person she was. The two were beginning to have little heart-to-heart talks on serious matters that were on Waterlily's mind, which her mother seemed to anticipate.

There was that lovely afternoon when they went from the camp for a walk, just Blue Bird and her three children, Waterlily, Ohiya, and Smiling One, who was now past two winters. Beyond the knoll they sat down to rest, and there was nobody and nothing in sight, only country. Blue Bird looked on her children fondly and said, "Now I am truly happy—surrounded by my children." And this she said because here was one of her rare opportunities to love them without limit, and to show them that she did. For in the larger family, where all adults acted parental toward all the children, they tried to be careful not to seem partial to any.

The beauty of the words, the stirring message they convey, are gifts of time, no less.

It is possible, of course, that I, being a writer, appreciate, and yes, *love*, these words with the sort of passion not necessarily shared by the average person, who, with his or her own set of interests does not feel the same sense of wonderment or excitement for mere words. Yet as I look around me at the world we have created, mostly by accident, but purposefully as well, it becomes apparent that without our stories, indeed, without our histories, collective and individual, we are little more than temporary shadows in a vast and nameless outer space. Without our stories, do we exist at all?

Each one of us is partially shaped by the words that surround us from day one until our final moment. Messages—positive, negative, confusing, damaging, life preserving—filter into our daily environment on a nonstop basis, messages composed of words. They are us; we are them.

As fundamental to our existence as the air we breathe, words are the building blocks of civilization, of time and place. On the prairie lands I grew up with, words tell of a time when regrettable events occurred; they tell of invasions, battles, and death.

From Black Elk, a holy man of the Ogalala Lakota/Sioux as told to John G. Neihardt for *Black Elk Speaks*:

It was the next summer, when I was 11 years old (1874) that the first sign of trouble came to us. Our band had been camping on Split-Toe Creek in the Black Hills, and from there we moved to Spring Creek, then to Rapid Creek where it comes out into the prairie.

He goes on to recount numerous moves and meetings, later saying:

The nights were sharp now, but the days were clear and still; and while we were camping there I went up into the Hills alone and sat a long while under a tree. I thought maybe my vision would come back and tell me how I could save that country for my people, but I could not see anything clear.

And finally, he says:

Crazy Horse stayed with about a hundred tepees on Powder, and in the middle of the Moon of the Snowblind (March) something bad happened there. It was just daybreak. There was a blizzard and it was very cold. The people were sleeping. Suddenly there were many shots and horses galloping through the village. It was the cavalry of the Wasichus, and they were yelling and shooting and riding their horses against the tepees. All the people rushed out and ran, because they were not awake yet and they were frightened.

The attack came in the early morning hours of March 16, 1876, when Colonel Reynolds with "six companies of cavalry attacked Crazy Horse's village."

If we could choose, many of us would wish these words away, pretend such times did not actually occur. Yet the words confirm the reality, and even though they are painful to acknowledge, it is important that we possess the history, that we have the stories to tell. For it is words that give life and meaning to our existence, and in underestimating their power and their purpose, we fail to appreciate the significance of the role they play.

Consider this, an optimistic message from Hiamovi, chief among the Cheyennes and the Dakotas, in his preface to *The Indians' Book: Authentic Native American Legends, Love and Music*, recorded and edited by Natalie Curtis:

There are birds of many colors—red, blue, green, yellow—yet it is all one bird. There are horses of many colors—brown, black, yellow, white—yet it is all one horse. So cattle, so all living things—animals, flowers, trees. So men: in this land where once were only Indians are now men of every color—white, black, yellow, red—yet all one people. That this should come to pass was in the heart of the Great Mystery. It is right thus. And everywhere there shall be peace.

Words of beauty, words that convey a depth of understanding and acceptance of the "Great Mystery." And what a magnificent story they tell.

ETERNAL SPRING

Within our stories, within our words, resides an eternal spring, in that inside each of us lies the unlimited power to craft a better tomorrow, one that more clearly expresses our deepest desires and secret yearnings, our dreams and visions and hopes. One that outlines the kind of world we want to live in; one that defines the world we so desperately want to leave behind for those who must follow in our footsteps, ever so willingly, ever so fearfully or bravely.

By keeping our stories alive and circulating, we preserve a strong sense of community, and in many ways we help prepare future generations for the inevitable challenges that lie ahead. They can learn from our mistakes; take heart in our undaunted courage; hold the wisdom of past ways close about them, like a protective shield against the onslaught of time, the onrush of fads, fantasy, and folly.

For surely the settlers of the 1800s, the Native Americans of the prairie lands, would hope we have all learned something from the past— the past that our stories will not let us forget or erase. And in their memory, let us show them honor by remembering to place a high value on their struggle to understand and to survive a changing world that seemed to be taking them down a very rocky path indeed.

We cannot change the past, but the past *can* change us, and within that sentiment lies additional cause, justifiable reason, to believe in an eternal spring.

In the words of an Ojibway elder and storyteller, Ignatia Broker, in her story about her great-great-grandmother, we can hear the wisdom, the hope, that is passed on to a young girl in preparation for a move made necessary "because there is another people who are fast coming. . . ."

Mother looked down at her fragile daughter, she who was much smaller than the other children of her age. She brushed Oona's black shining hair and lifted up the small oval face with the huge dark eyes.

"It is sad to be leaving, my Oona," said Mother, "but in one's life there are many times when one must leave a place of happiness for the unknown. I have done this many times, but the beauty of a life remains forever in the heart. You must remember the beauty that was here. Go, my daughter, and say the words of friendship to those who were your playmates."

A gust of wind, sweeping across the plain, threw into life

waves of yellow and blue and green. . . .

—OLE E. RÖLVAAG,

Giants in the Earth

COME AND GO

Now, as we take one final look, hopefully a lasting one, at the prairie that is so dear to my heart, at the lands that have been such a marvelous teacher, such a treasured friend, it is appropriate to consider the majestic blue skies and the sometimes daunting landscape from a broader perspective.

How does this well of prairie knowledge best fit into the limited number of years each of us has the privilege of living, into a life span that rarely exceeds 100 years in comparison with the virtual agelessness of the prairie?

Doubtless to say, you may discover this book as a young person, a retired person, or maybe as someone who plans to live forever—there really are a few people out there who refuse to concede defeat! So what can you derive from this book of prairie wisdom, regardless of your age, challenges, hopes and dreams, besides the concepts already revealed?

Initially, that nothing in life is wildly permanent. Even now, as I tell you about the marvels of the prairie, about its many charms, development plans threaten to encroach on the natural beauty of the native prairie; we cannot assume it will be with us indefinitely. "Progress" does take its toll—on all of us, on all parts of the globe. And so it is that in our efforts to make everything, including the prairie, conform to our endless demands and ongoing needs as a civilization, to our wishes, we may ultimately witness its demise. Of course, there are many who scoff at the very idea: Who would bother developing *that* part of the country, the part so rarely seen by others, when clearly the area lacks appeal?

But, almost inevitably, there comes a time when things do change, for better or worse, and though it may be impossible to envision at this point in our history, we all know from experience that it does happen, sometimes with tremendous surprise, agitation, and strife. One day it is entirely possible that we will wake up to find the prairie lands altered, made into something "more useful" or "more profitable."

To that end, there is tremendous merit in taking the time to view these lands with an eye for its distinct qualities—the ones that offer a unique perspective on the mysteries and magic of life.

THE MORNING LIGHT

First and foremost, we have learned that the prairie lands—the place, the culture, and the people—do not represent a nirvana; quite often the prairie's everlasting beauty is best found in the eye of the beholder.

And so it is that the morning light can indeed play tricks on those who wake up to the prairie each day. There are mornings when the land generates an expansive, wide-open feeling; other mornings, the vast, untamed area can feel empty and barren, overpowering in its magnitude, its starkness; sometimes the open spaces feel secure, warm, and inviting; and there are times when the flowing grasses, the intense sky, seem to mock all of mankind.

Captured within this landscape then is a poetic mix of extremes; like "The Velocity of Love," an enchanting musical piece by Suzanne

Where the Heart Resides

Ciani, the prairie can evoke feelings of peace, quiet despair, enraptured bliss, discontentment, and sudden restlessness—all at the same precise moment. The primary differential is what you bring to it: the morning light through which you view the immense space, vast distances, and the quality of sameness. An excellent barometer of your internal state, one that is difficult to deny, prairie spaces, indeed, prairie places, do not encourage escape from what is.

Rather, like a wise and knowing teacher, the open land seems to insist that each person find his or her way, there when needed but definitely not offering a utopian existence or a place to shrink from the challenges of life—thereby becoming less, not more. The prairie will not insulate you from yourself. No, not at all.

It will magnify your strengths and weaknesses, your silly side, your serious side, and the middle ground where you simply try to be yourself, try to discover who you are and what you are all about, forcing you to contend with the raw material you brought into the world, whatever that may be. But, on a paradoxical level, the prairie will also offer you comfort and solace against a harsh, often uncaring world—the one we all must take responsibility for creating.

Yet this is appropriate, as it has been said many times that "life is a paradox," and no matter how ill-equipped we feel to navigate our way through this sort of maze, we have very little choice. Certainly not if we are committed to a life of genuine self-discovery, something that requires energy, involvement, and a capacity to confront ourselves on a very primitive level. As we all know, personal truths can be sobering, if not unnerving and difficult to accept. But, in my mind at least, those people or places that give us the gift of self-knowledge represent the truest treasures of a lifetime because, in their presence, it is nearly always possible to feel the concern and caring that surrounds their "style," their belief in the amazing reservoir of human potential residing within each and every person.

As such, these sorts of influences, people or places or events, have a tendency to draw something—talents, abilities, feelings—from us that we scarcely knew existed. These are people who detect "truths" that we are unable to see ourselves; and by pushing our buttons, getting us riled up, believing in us for no apparent reason, or offering us very little room for excuses, we grow. And while we may hate it, find the process uncomfortable and annoying, even painful, it is through and because of these circumstances that true kindness and caring is discovered.

So, no matter how you view the prairie lands, no matter how you experience them—as a visitor, an inhabitant, or as a reader of this book—try to remember the gifts, the charms of the heart, readily offered by a people and a place that is barren yet bountiful; isolated and remote yet incredibly endearing; peaceful and freeing yet confining; poor yet rich. For this is a place that rarely allows people to settle for less than they are capable of being and becoming, and that, to me, is the greatest gift of all.

You see, nothing comes easy in a place "outsiders" love to ridicule, a place where the economy is often stagnant, where history announces the capacity for failure, where few secrets are kept—a place many must learn to love. Clearly, this is a place where nature is *the* force to reckon with, where people are reminded daily of their utter insignificance. And it is a place where evidence of a higher power is so vast, so clear, as to be somewhat intimidating. And perplexing. And humility-provoking. As a forty-seven-year resident of the area, the editor and publisher of *South Dakota Magazine*, put it when responding to interview questions:

"Anyone who can understand and appreciate the wonder of nature and yet deny a Higher Power is a champion of cynicism." His astute observation is a sharp reminder of the general ease with which modern-day society, indeed, those who comprise it, have allowed a disbelief in nearly everything previously held sacred and true to go by the wayside—without a fight.

Religion is clearly a personal preference, but the capacity to believe in something or someone other than what can be seen and witnessed firsthand is necessary to our survival as a species. Without a capacity to believe—in ourselves, in others, in unseen powers, in the basic goodness of womankind and mankind—our ship is halfway to the bottom. And as we were reminded by the movie *Titanic*, the ship can sink.

So, as the morning light eases its way into your bedroom, consider anew your internal state—how does it read, what does it tell you about yourself? Are you growing or are you dying? Are you truly awake or still asleep, at least partially? And are you fully cognizant of the world around you? Do you care? At all, or not even in the slightest?

What is the state of *your* soul? And, do *you* care?

GLAD TIDINGS

Yet as a testament to my belief in humanity, and in myself as well, I suggest, as a spokesperson for a land that has taught me a good deal about life and myself that the most painful lesson of all is this: *Your life's journey is not a predictable one; if you allow yourself room to grow, if you have the courage to grow when the opportunity presents itself, the web of life will take you to places you never dreamt of, rattle you in ways you thought impossible, move you to quiet despair and complete confusion,*

point you in directions that cause you to shake and shiver, push you to change your thinking, to alter your beliefs and assumptions, to admit defeat, to start over, time and time again. And to know, truly know from personal experience, that no one is immune from the hardships of life, its joys, its ups and downs, its puzzling manifestations, because what goes around . . . truly does come around.

So it is quite possible that the day will come when you will be required to leave your current, possibly happy, surroundings in a quest for greater knowledge, challenge, love, or purpose of heart. And as many have learned, to believe otherwise, to think, with false assurance, that you are immune from the normal pressures and learning experiences of life is to court disaster, to ensure a disruption of immense proportion.

A bit like the earthquake that was never supposed to happen, the blizzard that was not supposed to materialize, the drought that should not have occurred, the flood that was not anticipated, the prairie fire that should never have started, nature reminds us each day—if we will only listen—that we are not ultimate powers in the universe. Important, worthy of love and second chances, of course; capable of growth and change, of making mistakes yet surviving, absolutely; none of which, however, makes us invincible or omnipotent—it only makes us human. There is a difference.

But wondrously so, therein lies an element of optimism, reason to feel hopeful about the future. Not designed as perfect creatures, not intended to experience predictably safe or easy lives, we possess a built-in assurance for "success." On a spiritual and metaphysical level as well. And while this means accepting the temporary nature of life, as we know it, and believing in the need to "come and go" during the defining moments of our lives, we can, with courage and assurance, peer into the window of our hearts once again to discover a road map already drawn and marked, patiently waiting for our return.

We know the way back to our hearts; we have only lost sight of the path, a condition we can remedy even now, at this point in our history. A matter of letting more sunshine into our lives, of trusting our intuition—listening to it once again—of refusing to overlook intolerable conditions—being true to ourselves—and of knowing when to come, when to go: the task of a lifetime.

The key is to never say never. Stay open to surprise; anticipate change and challenge; be willing to listen to your heart once more—to *care*. Most of all, give your soul room to breathe. And if a deep wound should present itself, suddenly and with a mighty force, such as the recent death of my eighteen-year-old nephew, James Walker Bunn, those who knew and loved him must take heart from the incredible passion with which he lived each day. He lived knowing that life is always a precarious balance between the known and the unknown—between the expected and the unexpected. As his grandmother, Martha W. Bunn, put it, "Grandchildren are your heart."

So even though we all must "come and go" in a very literal sense, an inevitable consequence of our mortality, it is what we do with the time we have that counts. And if we are in touch with our hearts, with our spirituality, if we are true to our beliefs, a certain measure of immortality is bound to be ours. As evidenced by the lives we touch in a memorable and positive fashion, the love we give and leave behind is indeed . . . timeless.

EPILOGUE

Just as there may be a time to leave the prairie lands and continue a life's journey elsewhere, this is an opportune time for our nation, indeed, for our world, to consider its path. Is it time to change course, to rethink our direction or reevaluate priorities, to consider anew the heart of our nation?

Clearly, many of the most pressing questions will continue to go unanswered, even as we try, hope, and plan our way into the next century. But one thing is certain—in a place where life is reduced to the basics, where many of life's modern-day complexities fade, where one can still pull back the curtain to reveal natural, human elements, we are offered critical clues regarding our survival as a civilization. So, if there is one thing the prairie offers us at this point in our history, it is yet another chance to find our way back to our hearts: to a place we know but quietly abandoned in exchange for something called "progress." (Yet if we no longer listen to our hearts, how can we begin to know which is what? What appears to be progress may be ten steps backward or worse.)

In searching for the place that lies within, that place where your heart resides, it helps to view all places and stations in life as temporary stopping points where something of value can be learned; that way, you will know when it is time to go. For nothing subdues the heart more than to continue living a life that is without "heart," without true purpose that brings joy and meaning to your daily existence. By holding on to a path that has lost this quality, by not knowing when it is time to go, you destroy the power of heart in your life, letting your deep cynicism spill over into the lives of those around you. Ultimately, the choice is yours, but in the end, the effect is truly global.

IN APPRECIATION

The American Renaissance Chautauqua Companion Reader, presented by the Great Plains Chautauqua Society, Inc.

Beck, Charlotte Joko. *Now Zen.* San Francisco: HarperSan Francisco, 1995.

Brandt, Charles. *Meditations from the Wilderness.* Toronto: HarperCollins Publishers Ltd., 1997.

Broker, Ignatica. *Night Flying Woman: An Ojibway Narrative.* St. Paul, MN: Minnesota Historical Society, 1983.

Chaffee, John. *The Thinker's Way.* Boston: Little, Brown and Company, 1998.

Curtis, Natalie, ed. *The Indians' Book.* New York: Gramercy Books, 1994.

Deloria, Ella Cara. *Waterlily.* Lincoln, NE: University of Nebraska Press, 1988.

Herseth, Lorna Buntrock. *Autobiography.* Northfield: Fairway Foods, 1994.

Hopcke, Robert H. *There Are No Accidents.* New York: Riverhead Books, 1997.

Fanebust, Wayne. *Tales of Dakota Territory.* Sioux Falls: Mariah, 1994.

Hasselstrom, Linda, Gaydell Collier, and Nancy Curtis, eds. *Leaning into the Wind.* Boston and New York: Houghton-Mifflin (Marc Jaffe), 1997.

Heat-Moon, William Least. *PrairyErth.* Boston: Houghton-Mifflin (Peter Davison), 1991.

Madson, John. *Where the Sky Began.* Ames: Iowa State University Press, 1996. First edition, New York: Houghton-Mifflin, 1982.

Moore, Thomas. *Care of the Soul.* New York: HarperCollins, 1992.

Neihardt, John G. *Black Elk Speaks*. Reprinted by permission of the University of Nebraska Press. Copyright © 1932, 1959, 1972, by John G. Neihardt. Copyright © 1961 by the John G. Neihardt Trust.

Norris, Kathleen. *Dakota*. Boston and New York: Houghton-Mifflin, 1993.

Riley, Patricia, ed. *Growing up Native American*. New York: William Morrow & Company (Bill Adler), 1993.

Rölvaag, O. E. *Giants in the Earth*. New York: Harper & Row Perennial Library, 1927.

Swann, Brian and Arnold Krupat, eds. *I Tell You Now: Autobiographical Essays by Native American Writers*. Lincoln, NE: University of Nebraska Press, 1987.

Schuler, Harold H. *Pierre Since 1910*. Freeman, SD: Pine Hill Press, Inc. 1998.

Wee, Karen H. *The Book of Hearts*. Goodhue, MN: The Black Hat Press, 1993.

Wyman, Walker D, recorded by, from the original notes of Bruce Siberts. *Nothing but Prairie and Sky*. Norman and London: University of Oklahoma Press, 1954.

PERIODICALS

Adams, Robert. "Dakota Skies," *South Dakota Magazine*, March/April, 1996.

Lange, Cindy. "Pages of the Past," *South Dakota Magazine*, May/June, 1996.

McGinnis, Mark. "Elders of the Faith," *South Dakota Magazine*, November/December, 1995.

Peterson, Mark. "Wide Open Space," *South Dakota Magazine*, January/February, 1996.

The photos in this book and on the cover represent
Bob H. Miller's affinity with the prairie.
His work has appeared in *Zoom* magazine,
the Polaroid International Collection,
and the Midlands Invitational 1997 at the Joslyn Art Museum.
He is known for experimental large-scale photograms and
Polaroid manipulations.
Miller lives in Rapid City, South Dakota.

For more information about Bob H. Miller's work,
contact him at:

MILLER PHOTOGRAPHY
401 SOUTH STREET
RAPID CITY, SD 57701
(605) 343-6784

TO CONTACT THE AUTHOR

If you are interested in writing to Daisy Ann Hickman
regarding her book you may send E-mail to prairiewise@worldnet.att.net.

———————————

∽